FEAR IS THE FOE

FEAR IS THE FOE

*A Footslogger from
Normandy to the Rhine*

Stanley Whitehouse
and George B. Bennett

ROBERT HALE · LONDON

ISBN 0 7090 5704 0

Robert Hale Limited
Clerkenwell House
Clerkenwell Green
London EC1R 0HT

2   4   6   8   10   9   7   5   3   1

Photoset in North Wales by
Derek Doyle & Associates, Mold, Clwyd.
Printed in Great Britain by
St Edmundsbury Press Ltd, Bury St Edmunds, Suffolk.
Bound by WBC Book Manufacturers Limited,
Bridgend, Mid-Glamorgan.

Contents

Illustrations

PICTURE CREDITS

Imperial War Museum: 2–14.

Acknowledgements

I am deeply indebted to my good friend Les Davies and also to that old stalwart Bob Yates – alas, no longer with us – for their unstinting help and advice; and I must also thank R.G. (Bob) Carter, my old chum Arthur (Nobby) Clarke, and John Willoughby (the Royal Green Jackets) for providing valuable information on the First Bucks' D-Day role. Last, but not least, a special thank you to my wife Vee.

G.B.B.

This book is dedicated to Sergeant Percy Edmonds, Private Les (Beachy) Beach and Corporal Les (Shorty) Shorthouse, MM, fellow footsloggers who were never many yards from me during those hectic times. But of course I could never forget the thirty or so other platoon pals who fell by the wayside on that fearful trek from Normandy to the Rhine.

Stan Whitehouse

1   The Great Armada

As the tank landing craft stood out to sea, still a quarter of a mile or so from the Normandy beaches, I leaned on her rail and gazed in awe and astonishment. It was all too much to grasp. Seawards, as far as the eye could see, was a vast armada of ships of every shape and size: giant battleships and monitors, belching broadsides that sent one-ton shells far inland; stately cruisers adding their firepower from six-inch and eight-inch guns; nippy destroyers and frigates fussing round their charges, no doubt on the alert for prowling U-boats and E-boats; and a host of other vessels laden with men and equipment for this mightiest of all invasions – the Allied assault on Hitler's Fortress Europe.

Above us was the constant and deafening drone of aircraft as giant four-engined bombers, smaller Dakotas and agile fighter-bombers flew their deadly missions. Adding to the overall din was the screech and whine of shells – mostly heading shorewards, though some came our way – the sudden swish as mattresses of rockets leapt from their barges, and the steadier, more incessant chatter of machine-guns and small arms fire.

My unit, the 1st Buckinghamshire Battalion, the First Bucks to the old sweats, a territorial battalion of the Oxfordshire and Buckinghamshire Light Infantry, was part of No. 6 Beach Group, an independent command attached in its turn to the 3rd British Infantry Division (I Corps), comprising mortar men, anti-tankers, engineers and other specialist personnel. Our task, in conjunction with No. 5 Beach Group, was to secure designated areas just beyond Sword beach, to be used as fuel and ammunition dumps. C Company, to which I belonged, was also detailed to hold the Caen Canal Bridge and locks and later to guard the dumps against enemy infiltration (see Appendix).

Below the 3rd Division's red and blue triangular shoulder

flash we wore a strange and puzzling patch bearing the joined initials JP. Only recently did I discover that this signified we were an independent brigade (the 162nd) and the initials were those of Major-General J.H.T. Priestman, the original commander of the parent territorial division.

D-Day was originally scheduled for 5 June 1944 and we had accordingly boarded LCT 303 at Gosport the previous day. But because of bad weather the invasion was postponed for twenty-four hours, and we eventually sailed on the evening of 5 June. Once at sea officers and senior NCOs received more detailed information and maps showing for the first time the correct Normandy place names.

After a rough crossing in choppy seas, whipped up by a blustery wind, we hove to just offshore at dawn on the 6th and awaited our turn to disembark on Sword beach. Before sailing we were given anti-seasickness tablets, which must have worked because I had poor sea legs yet suffered no ill effects from the heaving ship. However, for several days after landing some of us experienced the weird sensation of a moving horizon.

A large assault craft laden to the gunwales with commandos wearing their famous green berets came up from behind to overtake us, and waves and shouts of greeting and encouragement were exchanged.

'Look at the cheeky buggers – they're fishing!' one of our lads called out. Sure enough they had what appeared to be makeshift fishing lines dangling over the boat's side. We were dumbfounded and had to admire the coolness and the style of these men who were going into the cauldron to blaze a trail for the rest of us. With shouts of 'Good luck' on either side the Green Berets sped towards the beach.

'Christ! Look at that,' someone near me shouted, and following the direction of his finger I saw a heavy bomber ablaze and hurtling earthwards. It hit the ground some way inland amid a huge pall of black oily smoke. I failed to see any parachutes opening.

'Look over there,' someone else called, and I saw another plane – it seemed to be a fighter – trailing the merest wisp of smoke as it gradually lost height, obviously in trouble. It crashed into the sea and again I searched in vain for parachutes.

'Hey! Take a look at that,' called an excited squaddie, pointing to starboard. A large transport ship had received a direct hit that had ripped out its entrails. The ship seemed to lurch and smaller craft rushed in to pick up survivors bobbing about in the water.

And so the battle raged as we switched our gaze from one spectacular scene to another, held spellbound and stupefied by the scale and ferocity of it all. Ashore I could make out men edging forward, with one or two stumbling or falling, and a carpet of corpses seemed to surround one stubborn enemy pillbox. Then a small naval craft dashed close in and pumped shells into the strongpoint until it was silenced by well-aimed shots through the gun slits. These smaller naval guns also blasted away at beach summer-houses, ripping off roofs and shutters to unveil fortified pillboxes that were causing mayhem among our lads wading ashore.

'Permission to take bodies aboard, sir,' requested an able seaman.

'Not a good idea,' replied the ship's officer. 'We'll collect them on the way back.' We peered over the side and were horrified to see more than a dozen bodies floating limply, heads down, and bumping against the side of the ship before heading out to sea. They were wearing life-jackets which had obviously kept them afloat.

'Bloody hell's bells!' someone near me exclaimed. We looked at each other, and my mates' faces had taken on an expression I had never seen before. Stark reality had hit me like a cold douche. So far I had regarded the cross-Channel invasion as a noble crusade, a grand adventure to recount later to my mates back home over a pint; and in our squat and sturdy LCT I had felt insulated and relatively secure. Now my stomach had knotted and I was gripped by a fearful dread. That could have been me floating down there. I forced myself to look at the bodies again as they drifted away on the heavy swell. An hour ago they were full of vitality and raring to go; now they were the flotsam of war. Thank goodness they remained facing downwards, preventing our seeing their agonized expressions, or, indeed, whether they had any faces at all. Swirls of blood surrounded several bodies as they rocked and heaved in the unfriendly sea.

It puzzled me why they should all, without exception, float face down. I had assumed that a life-jacket would keep a man's face upwards. If I were wounded and fainted would I drown before being rescued? Were some of those floating away merely unconscious and drowning? I posed this question to Mad Geordie, who stood beside me.

'Why aye, man. One bugger looked up at me and winked. He'll be back home in Blighty by morning,' he said laughing. I was initially shocked at such remarks about our dead boys, but when one or two others standing nearby joined in the laughter I realized their attitude was probably right. Those lads in the sea were goners and all the pious words in the world would not bring them back. It was better to laugh than to cry and thereby bury the gnawing fear deep in our minds. We were young with strong nerves, enabling us to face these horrors squarely. But after days and weeks of such scenes – and maybe worse – would we still be able to shrug them off? Time would tell. Even before joining up I had wondered how I would react to the horrors of war and having to shoot fellow human beings. In my youthful innocence – I was still almost five months short of my eighteenth birthday – I had imagined that conditions would be similar to those of the earlier conflict of 1914–18 with its deep muddy trenches and months of static warfare. I had reached the conclusion that the fighting would continue for ten years or more and that with a little luck I would be able to endure it, and with a little more luck survive.

At least the sight of those bodies had a salutary effect and dispelled any lingering complacency. The fun and games and the jolly manoeuvres were over. It was time to remember our training, otherwise we too might be floating face down in the water.

Leaning on the ship's rail I looked back with some misgivings at the twists and turns my life had taken over the past year or two. After leaving school early – thanks to a letter I had forged, supposedly from my mother, saying I was urgently needed at home to contribute to the family's dwindling finances – I joined the local ordnance factory, churning out munitions. But the tedium of tapering an endless stream of Sten gun firing pins drove me to distraction and I craved a soldier's life so passionately that I tampered with the date of birth on my ration book. In an instant I had aged two years, becoming eighteen (the minimum age for enlistment), enabling me to join the Ox and Bucks, my dad's old regiment, when in fact I had just celebrated my sixteenth birthday. I assured my anxious parents that I had joined the boys' army and would not see action until I was eighteen.

The army medical held no terrors for me. I had led an active life, with running and boxing among my sports, and had been blessed with a good physique, being 5 feet 8 inches tall and having wiry, black hair, big brown eyes and a snub nose. Sixteen weeks' hard grind transformed me from a hesitant youth into a confident soldier, eager for action. But looking towards Sword beach, with its general tumult and violence, I began to have doubts about my confidence and eagerness.

'All hands below decks except Bren gunners and their number twos,' came a strident voice over the ship's tannoy. Private Les Shorthouse (Shorty) and I, our section's Bren team, were placed forward on the main deck, while other Bren teams were scattered strategically around the ship. We engaged several enemy planes shooting up the beach and ships lying offshore, but had no luck. The few German aircraft we did see seemed to have little stomach for the fight and failed to press home their attacks with any determination. It was comforting and reassuring to see that the Allied air forces' umbrella of fighters had kept the Luftwaffe at bay, thereby gaining air supremacy over the whole invasion area.

'All Brens cease firing,' came the tannoy voice again. 'Save your ammo for the landing.' That made sense to us. Shorty and I went below, leaving the matelots on the top structure to ward off trouble with their twin Vickers.

Below decks I found the atmosphere unreal and deceptive. Some squaddies were playing cards with reckless abandon, as though there would be no tomorrow. Perhaps they had a premonition. Hundreds of pounds in our newly-acquired currency were being won and lost on the turn of a single card. Other soldiers sang hymns with great gusto, but I had no inclination for cards or hymns and quickly pushed my way back up the companionway and into the fresh air.

Major Johnny Kaye, our company commander, and his batman were in full battle gear, as though about to disembark. The batman, coincidentally also Johnny Kay, but without the final 'e', a small, weedy chap we called Little Johnny, looked ready to collapse under the weight of his equipment, which no doubt included his officer's personal gear. His pockets were crammed full, he carried a bandolier of ammunition about his neck and his pouches were bulging with grenades.

'Are we off then?' I asked him.

'Only company HQ personnel,' he answered. 'I think we're running late and this bloody nutter wants to go ashore and see what's going on.' And he rolled his eyes towards Major Kaye. A huge steel raft came alongside and began receiving tanks and trucks from the belly of our ship. The major and his party of about ten followed the vehicles aboard the raft and with enemy shelling erupting geysers of water on either side of them they headed for the beach.

The thunder of battle continued unabated as more planes droned overhead – some returning from missions – the big naval guns continued to roar and fresh troops swarmed ashore. And all the while we remained kicking our heels almost within spitting distance of Sword beach. But I was in no hurry to join in the fracas. The beach still looked unhealthy and German artillery seemed to have the range. Better to let the navy and the Brylcreem boys sort out a few more Jerries before we land, I thought.

Behind us I spotted that old warhorse HMS *Rodney*, looking a little lopsided with all her big guns forward. My brother Ray was a marine aboard her and at that moment we seemed so close and yet so far apart. As the battleship and the nearby monitor HMS *Roberts* fired their massive guns at targets miles inland they seemed to roll with the recoil.

Up top I was mesmerized by the whole gigantic, terrifying show, of which I felt such an insignificant part. Occasionally a sailor would sidle over and chat; these young matelots appeared so calm and unruffled, though I guessed that deep down they were just as scared as me but were doing their utmost to hide it.

Darkness engulfed us, but there was no let-up in the struggle. On the contrary it seemed more ferocious than ever and certainly more spectacular, with 'flaming onions' and tracers stitching the inky blackness, while searchlights from hundreds of ships continually threshed about the sky and the beachhead. I clearly saw a small plane coming over us very low – it was well below the searchlights' probing beams. Suddenly every gun in the vicinity opened up and in desperation the pilot twisted and turned to evade the murderous fire, first heading out to sea and then turning inland. The aircraft finally crashed, striking the rear of a ship near us, with one wing dipping into the sea and the other resting on the deck. Searchlights homed in and then there was a brief but ominous silence: the plane's wings bore friendly black and white identification stripes.

'Christ! It's one of ours,' exclaimed someone behind me.

I found a corner down below and despite the incessant racket managed a catnap before being roused at dawn by the order 'Get dressed.' In future those two words would churn up my stomach and strike terror into my heart. They meant that soon we would be 'eye-balling the enemy'.

The steel raft drew alongside us again and after tanks and scout cars had been transferred from the LCT fifty or sixty of us followed, dragging trailers or handcarts with us. These sturdy metal carts (one per platoon) were about five feet by four feet and two feet deep, and had pneumatic tyres and a T-shaped handle for easy pulling. They were loaded with 303 ammunition, Piat and mortar bombs and grenades, and were expected to float if we got into difficulties, though I had my doubts.

As we headed shorewards I stood alongside Sergeant Percy Edmonds – Old Edmonds as we affectionately called him. At our first encounter, with the First Bucks at Ayr, when I was still sixteen, he looked me up and down.

'Whitehouse,' he said, 'if you're eighteen, I'm the Aga bleedin' Khan.'

I tried to look hurt at being called a liar, but from that moment a rapport developed between us and I came to admire him immensely.

The sergeant, from Buckinghamshire, was a Dunkirk veteran and at thirty-nine rather old for an infantryman. On returning from Dunkirk he had hurried home to his worried wife and teenage son and after a warm greeting had slung his rifle and equipment in the front room and gone upstairs for a bath. Before he could undress there was a loud bang and he flew down to find his son lying dead – shot through the head while examining the rifle. The lad was sixteen; maybe that was why I had not fooled the old soldier about my age. He had a wonderful head of hair, but it was pure white. No wonder. Now, as we headed towards the Normandy beach, the air charged with the furious din and the pungent fumes of war, I felt reassured standing beside the calm, unflappable Old Edmonds.

I overheard our second-in-command telling the sergeant that

German heavy guns had our particular sector of beach zeroed in, making it too hot for us, and we were now landing a little further west on Juno beach, in the Canadian sector. Once clear of the beaches we were to skirt the town of Ouistreham and work our way towards the lighthouse at the mouth of the River Orne and the Caen Canal. I could make out the lighthouse over to our left; surprisingly its white tower, ideal as an enemy observation post, was still intact, despite the heavy naval and air pounding.

As the motor-driven raft chugged nearer the beach small naval craft, like broody hens fussing over their chicks, darted in and out, calmly attending to their duties, quite oblivious to the noise and carnage around them. A DD tank (Duplex Drive and fitted with 'skirts' to enable it to swim ashore) had drowned in the shallows; so too had other vehicles which were being steadily lapped by the incoming waves.

Our raft ploughed into the sand and we jumped out to land knee-deep in water. At least we were able to keep most of our equipment dry, unlike squaddies from other units who apparently got a soaking. A number of landing craft following us beached on sand bars and disembarking troops, after walking just a few paces, disappeared in six or seven feet of water. I later heard that some men were issued with condoms (French letters to us in those days) which they fitted over the muzzles of their rifles to keep out the salt water.

Major Kaye and company HQ personnel, all looking dispirited and strained, were at the water's edge to meet us. It was evident that they had found the going tough since landing.

'Get off the beach as quickly as you can,' ordered the major. 'We'll RV later. Little Johnny will show you where. Come on now chaps. Chop, chop!' And the major clapped his hands to urge us on.

Men of the King's (Liverpool) Regiment, whose cap badge sported a prancing horse, were from No. 5 Beach Group, in the first wave, and had borne the brunt of the initial fighting in this particular sector, suffering heavy casualties. Undeterred by individual disasters, the men had gallantly pressed forward to eliminate shoreline strongpoints and gain a firm foothold. While their officers were attending an O Group (an officers' meeting) in a beach-house it received a direct hit, killing most of them. The effect on morale right through the battalion must have been catastrophic.

As we struggled from the water's edge with our platoon's heavily laden handcart, hauled by Shorty, Les Beach (Beachy), Eddie Jolliffe, Ken Ware and me, Eddie shouted, 'Christ! Look out lads!' I stared aghast. About twenty-five to thirty Germans with smoke-blackened faces and eyes starkly white, looking wild and angry, were charging towards us. We fumbled desperately for our weapons, slung awkwardly around our necks to enable us to push the cursed handcart. Fear turned to bewilderment. Now they were among us – and past us, chased by an alert Tommy, who was herding these prisoners on to the raft we had just vacated. We looked at each other, immensely relieved and rather sheepish at our reaction to seeing the enemy for the first time. I glanced back at the POWs huddled in the big steel raft and felt a tinge of envy. Their troubles were over; ours were about to begin.

While we heaved and pushed to free the cart's wheels from a particularly deep rut Les Beach called out excitedly, 'Stan, Stan, take a look at that,' and he nodded towards a small and rather crudely written sign stuck in the sand which read 'Nan Beach' (a sub-sector beach). Now Beachy's wife was Nancy, or Nan for short, and seeing her name there, so far from home, visibly upset him. He was a highly emotional Welshman and remained deep in thought for some time. Beachy suffered badly with varicose veins which caused him to hobble and wince at times, and he should never have been in the infantry.

We passed clusters of angle iron, metal stakes and other obstacles, known as Rommel's 'asparagus' – some now twisted into weird shapes by the shelling – planted as part of Hitler's Fortress Europe to thwart invaders from the sea. A little way off I saw a flail tank, lying useless with a severed track. These tanks were among the assortment of specialized armoured vehicles developed by General Hobart and his team of experts and became known as Hobart's 'funnies' or the 'can-openers of Normandy' because of their ability to overcome enemy obstacles and open the way inland. The flails exploded mines in their path by pounding the ground with a series of whirling chains. Other tanks carried bridging gear or steel 'carpets' which, when laid in soft sand prevented wheeled vehicles becoming bogged down; and the petard had a giant mortar for destroying concrete strongpoints. Perhaps Hobart's most lethal weapon was the Crocodile flame-thrower with a range of more than a hundred yards. These 'funnies' were to prove a godsend to us squaddies and must have saved many lives, though we later heard that they were spurned by the Americans, much to their regret, at bloody Omaha beach, further along the coast.

A shell burst a few yards away, but most of its killing power was neutralized by the soft sand. However, Private Taffy Jones keeled over with a nasty gash in his shoulder. I was amazed to see a pretty battle-dressed female nurse dash out from a motley group crouching nearby. She pulled him into the shelter of a beached landing craft and quickly dressed his wound.

'The lucky bugger,' someone near me muttered. 'I wouldn't mind copping some shrapnel if a dolly bird was going to drool all over me.'

It was tough work hauling our ammunition cart and we paused for a breather and to allow some tanks through. For just a brief moment I was able to take stock of the scene – an ever-changing scene that was mind-boggling. Our seaborne assault was now well under way as the colossal, monstrous tide of men and equipment, wave after wave of them, continued to spill onto the beaches, where organized confusion reigned. Occasionally individual progress was briefly checked by shell and mortar bursts but the overall momentum was maintained. Orders and counter-orders to various outfits wafted across the sands and beach marshals, perhaps more vulnerable than most on these naked shores, did their best to bring some semblance of sanity to the disorder. Above and beyond it all was the almost continuous roar of aircraft and the screech of incoming shells from our navy boys.

Some yards offshore a large LCI (Landing Craft Infantry), with an accommodation ladder running down each side, was disgorging its passengers. One ladder suddenly collapsed and more than a dozen men were flung into the sea. Encumbered with heavy packs they floundered out of their depth and were in danger of drowning. We felt compelled to help and made a move in their direction, but a beach marshal stopped us.

'Get off this bloody beach,' he barked. 'They'll be taken care of.' Sure enough, eight naked men – navy commandos, I believe – dashed to their rescue, each carrying a stout rope, the other end of which was firmly held by a naked anchorman on the beach.

We continued to hump our cart, sweating and cursing as we pushed and pulled to extricate its wheels from the softer sand higher up the beach.

'God knows what will happen to this bloody lot – and us – if a stray bullet lands among the ammo,' said Shorty between gasps. The consequences were too grim to bear thinking about, though on reflection having the cart to push kept our minds occupied and was perhaps a blessing in disguise.

Further on we met an odd young chap dressed in khaki but sporting an RAF shoulder flash. Around his waist was a steel hoop from which several sandbags hung. Also attached to the hoop was a thin cable which rose into the air and held a small barrage balloon. Amid the frenetic activity he looked strangely out of place walking up and down the beach.

'What's going on then, matey?' I asked, trying to be friendly.

'A deterrent to low-flying aircraft,' he answered. (Much later I learned that the balloons were in fact intended to mark the beach exits for vehicular traffic.) Just then the beach marshal approached us again, looking angry.

'Don't hang about. Clear off this bloody beach. And you,' he said, pointing to the airman, 'cut that blasted balloon loose. The enemy artillery are using them as markers. And tell your mates to do the same. Hurry, hurry, you dozy bastards!'

So that's why the German shelling was so accurate. No wonder the beach marshal was annoyed, fearful of shells crashing about his ears. Mention of enemy artillery gave us renewed strength and we quickly left the beach, though not before I had glanced behind me once more. My view was partially impeded by dense smoke coming from several burning vehicles, but it was a heartening, uplifting sight to see more and more troops and equipment pouring ashore and the wounded being transferred in small craft to hospital ships out at sea. Apparently the whole stupendous operation, despite the hiccups, had been more successful than our top brass had dared hope, and casualties were not as heavy as they had feared. After all, the Germans, reputed to be thorough and efficient, had spent four years preparing their defences.

While we rested again I spotted two squaddies cowering under a hedge, quivering and obviously in a state of severe shock after some recent ordeal.

'Been a bit rough, fellas?' I asked, hoping to console them. Not a glance came my way; they stared hard at the ground, shaking all over. So far I had managed to conquer my own fears, real though they were at times, especially when confronted with dead bodies. Naively I still regarded the invasion as a big adventure. Death or mutilation was the lot of the other fellow, and in meeting these two shell-shocked squaddies I was at a loss what to say or do and could only wonder what terrible calamity had reduced them to such a wretched state.

Fear, stark overpowering fear, can play devilish tricks with men's minds, as I discovered most convincingly during training exercises in Scotland earlier in the war. Ginger Thompson, my Bren gun oppo along with Private Slack (Slacky), was gripped by an all-pervading, ungovernable fear, convinced that he would die in the army. Nothing I said could dissuade him from this morbid premonition. Whenever he sensed danger, or the prospect of being shipped overseas, he skipped camp, only to be returned by the MPs. Before our last major scheme, deep in the Scottish Highlands with live ammunition, he had nowhere to run and reported sick, whereupon the MO gave him a sick note in red ink, signifying that he was a malingerer, and earning him a two-hour punishment drill; he was highly incensed.

On the scheme we found an ideal site for our Bren and were firing furiously when a mortar bomb fell between my two oppos. Slacky had his head blown off and Ginger rolled across my legs, mortally wounded. I had been refilling the Bren mags in a shallow crater a foot or two away and miraculously escaped unhurt. The MO dashed over and as he leaned down Ginger clawed at his face, leaving bloody streaks on the officer's cheeks.

'I suppose you'll be giving me red ink for this, you bastard!' he snarled. Ginger died later in hospital, his premonition of an early death sadly coming true.

Now, as I looked down at the two broken-spirited squaddies, shaking uncontrollably beneath the hedge, I thought of poor Ginger Thompson and his tormented mind that had driven him almost to the point of dementia. Pangs of fear gripped my belly. Would I end up like that? Surely not, and yet .... My throat dried up, making it difficult to swallow. Feeling ill at ease I was glad when we moved on.

We were at the rear of the column, crossing a rough football pitch, when a shell exploded a few yards from the leaders. The call for stretcher-bearers went up from the front. As Private Ray Cheadle, our chief stretcher-bearer, had his stretchers on the top of our handcart, we felt obliged to help him and dashed with stretchers to the scene of the commotion to find Privates

Palmer and Hutchinson lying wounded. Palmer had a huge gash in the thigh and was writhing in pain and losing blood, so we tended him first. I glanced across at Hutch who looked pale, though I could see no wound or blood.

'Be with you in a minute, Hutch,' called Ray as he stemmed the flow of blood from Palmer's thigh. Hutch merely nodded and gave a wry smile. When we eventually moved over to him he was dead.

'What the hell?' said the puzzled Ray.

'Was it the blast?' I asked. We had come to this conclusion when Sergeant Edmonds approached and, equally puzzled, bent down and lifted Hutch's left arm. We saw two tiny holes in his side where shrapnel had pierced his ribcage and struck vital organs. Shorty and I stretchered him to a road where we left him with the lads of the Pioneer Corps. The Pioneers had the most unenviable task of all, collecting and registering the dead. Bodies left lying around were bad for morale and the Pioneers went about their macabre work quietly and without fuss, discreetly laying the dead out of sight. They were truly unsung heroes.

We moved off the football pitch into a long, straight lane flanked by high hedges interspersed with an occasional tree or house. Toiling with our handcart, we had fallen about twenty yards behind the rest when without warning a Spandau machine-gun to our front opened up. Instantly the whole column went to ground and word filtered back that our Bren carriers were dealing with opposition up ahead.

'Bloody good luck to 'em,' puffed Eddie Jolliffe in his rich West Country brogue. We hugged the grass verge in the cool shade of a beech hedge, waiting for the signal to continue.

Burrp, burrp.

'There it is again,' muttered Kenny Ware, his big eyes rolling from side to side as though he expected someone to leap out on us. A few beech leaves fluttered down on our shoulders as we lay behind the cart. Another short Spandau burst was accompanied by the strange, delicate buzzing sound and more leaves fell. Shorty looked up into the hedge.

'What's causing these bleedin' leaves to fall on us?' he asked, getting to his feet and raising his rifle. Fear gave us extra energy and the rest of us jumped to our feet, facing the hedge. The enemy machine-gun fired yet again and we distinctly heard the peculiar buzzing noise about our heads and saw the leaves cut from the hedge.

'Bloody hell!' shouted Beachy. 'That Spandau's got us lined up. He must be able to see us.' I realized then that the strange buzzing was the noise of bullets whipping through the hedge just above us and slicing the beech leaves. With our handcart a veritable time bomb on wheels we were apprehensive and undecided what to do. As we dithered our minds were made up for us by a bizarre incident. Just across the way stood a cottage from which an old lady emerged carrying a small case. She glanced at us, looked up and down the lane and then came over and placed the case a few feet from us. Hobbling as fast as her rickety legs could carry her, she headed towards the beach.

'Christ!' gasped Kenny. 'That case could be a bomb!' We had heard rumours of German paras dressed as nuns and this, coupled with our recent traumas, had us deeply worried. Our training had not covered such contingencies.

'Run for it!' shouted Eddie, and crouching low we scurried towards our mates relaxing up ahead.

'What's up? Jerry ain't behind us, is he?' someone asked. We were too ashamed to tell the truth and merely dropped down among the other lads. Hearing the commotion, Sergeant Edmonds came over.

'What's going on? Why have you left the handcart back there?'

'An old lady just came out of that cottage and dumped that case in front of us Sarge,' said Kenny, pointing down the lane.

'Yeah, and we think it's a bomb,' added Eddie excitedly.

'Yer what?' exploded Old Edmonds, looking as though he would shoot us on the spot. 'An old lady has put her suitcase down and you lot have run away?'

'Well why didn't she take it with her?' I chipped in. For all his bravado dear Old Edmonds had no intention of checking the case. He fired his Sten at it and as the bullets ripped into it the case bumped and bounced several feet down the lane before bursting open to reveal slippers, hairbrushes and ladies' 'smalls', which lay scattered over the lane.

'Now get back and bring that bloody cart here,' ordered the sergeant, giving us a withering look. Just then an anxious Lieutenant Soulsby, our platoon commander, appeared.

'What's going on Sergeant?' he asked. 'Why all the shooting?'

'You wouldn't believe me if I told you sir,' muttered old Percy half to himself. 'Everything's fine sir. One of our lads thought he saw a sniper in a tree. A false alarm sir.' We returned to our cart feeling rather sheepish, but grateful to dear Old Edmonds for not spilling the beans to our officer.

We finally reached our first objective – a bridge over the Caen Canal, near the lighthouse, and from the shelter of an overturned tram I could see demolition charges strapped to the bridge's metal framework. Were the Germans lying in wait, ready to blow the bridge as we crossed? The answer soon came when British commandos on the far side called out that they had neutralized the charges, prompting us to hurry across and join them. Apparently they had been left behind to deal with the bridge explosives and we felt much better for seeing them. Though few in numbers, they looked tough and highly efficient and proved a real boost to our morale.

Now fired up, we charged with fixed bayonets into a copse alongside the canal on our first 'seek out and kill' sortie, with Major Kaye, cool and in complete control, supervising the operation. When he was satisfied that the enemy had left he ordered us to dig in and camouflage up.

Soon darkness fell and with it came a measure of relief, if not security. It had been a long, gruelling and eventful day – and I had survived it.

2 'No Dunkirk This Time'

For several weeks after the D-Day landings the battle for Normandy developed into an untidy, messy, slogging match, with meagre territorial gains – certainly in our sector. Evidently our top brass had been far too optimistic in expecting a speedy break-out from the bridgehead. But the build up of men and equipment continued, so much so that the beaches became congested and an easy target for enemy artillery and sporadic Luftwaffe raids. One wag reckoned that skyscrapers would have to be built to accommodate everyone.

Our first night in France was spent patrolling and helping engineers stretch camouflage scrim netting from tree to tree in an attempt to mask the canal bridge, which had attracted enemy shelling every time a vehicle approached. Later some of us lay along the banks of the River Orne in case German patrols sneaked over. It was unnerving lying in pitch darkness, unable to see more than a couple of feet ahead and with ears strained to the utmost for the slightest sound. Suddenly we heard faint splashing and several ghostly figures emerged from the water. I felt jumpy and was about to open fire when a voice called softly:

'British – British Paras. Don't shoot.'

'It may be a trick,' someone near me whispered excitedly. But I thought I recognized a north country accent, and in fact they were our boys, dropped miles off course behind enemy lines in the early hours of D-Day, and now returning to our lines after creating untold confusion further inland.

Some of our unit stayed on the far side of the bridge, ferreting out snipers and dashing to wherever small groups of Germans were spotted, but one enemy patrol eluded our pickets and shot up a front aid post, killing a number of wounded commandos.

For some time German snipers continued to be a menace,

crawling up to our lines at night and preparing excellent 'hides' that were difficult to locate. Their prime target was our officers, who eventually met guile with guile by making themselves as inconspicuous as possible, removing epaulettes and discarding binoculars, clipboards and other tell-tale signs of authority and carrying rifles instead of revolvers.

I had my first taste of digging for Teller mines on the track crossing the Point de Siège, the area between the canal and the river. The mines had already been found and marked by another platoon, but inexplicably had never been removed. It was night-time and while I probed with my small bayonet, Shorty stood nearby with his Sten at the ready and Beachy, a little way off in case I triggered a mine, held a rope and hook. Gasping like a stranded fish I probed with steel and fingers, my face streaming sweat and the saliva mysteriously disappearing from my mouth. It was a tricky, nerve-tingling job hooking the mines on to Beachy's long rope and pulling them out and I felt I was entitled to swagger a little as I carried them back for defusing. Back home we had been thoroughly brainwashed about mines and booby-traps and were urged to refrain from jumping into recently-vacated German foxholes, or approaching their corpses, for fear of fiendish boobies.

I also had my first terrifying experience of the enemy's *Nebelwerfers*, multi-barrelled mortars, nicknamed 'Moaning Minnies' because of their frightful wailing sound in flight. This banshee howl, created by an ingenious siren in the tail, had us all cringing in our 'slitters'. Landing as they did in clusters, their fragmentation effect was tremendous.

Mysterious fires broke out at night in the ammunition dumps near the beach and we had to patrol the area constantly, searching for saboteurs. Beachy, Shorty and I were patrolling the beach when enemy shelling began. We dived into a hollow alongside another group of about twenty squaddies, lying in a neat line, and when the shelling stopped we three stood up.

'How the hell can they sleep through this racket?' asked Beachy, nodding towards the prone figures. We looked a little closer and realized they were all dead.

One day I watched two Spitfires chasing a German fighter-bomber backwards and forwards over the beachhead. The German was skilful and achieved his aim of flattening out and dropping his bombs on the ammunition dump. The result was spectacular as ammunition and fuel stacked in adjacent fields received direct hits. I saw a DUKW (an amphibian lorry) lift high into the air and land upside down. Fires and explosions followed and our company – except for a couple of Bren gunners guarding the bridge – were ordered to help fight the blaze. Supervising operations was our platoon commander, Lieutenant Soulsby, a young, keen, dashing officer who looked rather comical with two prominent front teeth and a behind that protruded when he walked. He ordered us to move a lorry blocking the only road in and out of the dump. Private Eddie Jolliffe of Bristol immediately jumped into the cab and began backing the vehicle out. More bombs rained down, forcing us to take cover. When we emerged we were horrified to see that a huge tree had been uprooted and flung across the lorry's cab, killing Eddie. We could do nothing for my mate; he had to stay there until a crane was summoned to remove the tree.

Meanwhile the fires continued raging around the ammunition as we fought a losing battle with shovelfuls of sandy soil. One particular stack of shells was causing concern and eventually we backed off from the heat and the flying 303 bullets exploding nearby. A Jeep skidded to a halt and out jumped the enterprising Lieutenant Soulsby.

'Whitehouse, Beach, Cheadle,' he bawled, 'grab these.' And he handed each of us a small fire extinguisher. We hit the plungers and began spraying the shells from about fifteen yards, the limit of the jet.

'Oh for Christ's sake, get closer,' he ordered, and so saying he got behind us and pushed us to within a couple of feet of the burning stack.

'And bloody stop there or you'll be in serious trouble,' he barked, turning away to organize something else. To an infantryman shells are big, nasty things that blow you to pieces when they land nearby. The intricacies of timers and primers meant nothing to us. These shells were stuffed with explosives and surrounded by flames; enough to make any squaddie wince.

We were greatly relieved when the appliances ran out of water and we turned to move away. But our energetic lieutenant pounced again.

'Come on, tear the cylinders apart and stack the shells under that hedge.' Each shell was in its own cardboard cylinder and it was these cylinders that were burning. Lieutenant Soulsby set an example by ripping open the packaging and carrying the shells to safety. There was no way out; we had no alternative but to help. To give the young officer his due, he was unmoved by all about him and led from the front. As we toiled, placing each shell under the hedge, Ray Cheadle suddenly grabbed his Sten.

'Look out!' he shouted. 'One of the bastards is coming this way.' I looked up and was shocked to see a German-helmeted figure, silhouetted against the flames, approaching us. I dived for my rifle and a voice calmly asked in a broad English dialect:

'How are you chaps doin'?' It was Old Edmonds, our beloved sergeant.

'Christ Sarge, I nearly shot you,' said Ray angrily. 'Why the Jerry hat?'

'I've lost my bugger diving about and you need something with all this shit flying about,' said the sergeant, completely unperturbed.

'But it's a bit chancy Sarge, wearing a bloody Jerry hat, ain't it?' I chipped in.

'Well, I've put the bugger on back'ards. A Jerry wouldn't wear his helmet back to front, would he, sonny?' His answer left us speechless.

We were kept busy all through the night, the glow from the fires attracting the enemy's long-range and medium guns. The constant screech and whine of incoming shells had us diving to the ground so often that as dawn broke we were experts at recognizing from the various whistles and whines where the shells were about to strike. Almost arrogantly we merely flinched and ducked and cursed at most missiles, but when we heard just the dreaded rush of air – no whistle or screech – indicating a hit or very near miss, our speed at hitting the ground was something to behold.

At dawn the shellfire eased and our supply trucks began rolling slowly into the dump zone. Although fatigued almost to the point of dropping, we were given no respite.

'Come on lads, help unload this truck,' called Lieutenant Soulsby.

'Jesus bloody wept,' exploded Shorty, 'I'm absolutely parched. I couldn't spit a tanner.'

'I'm the same,' I croaked. 'A brew would go down well, wouldn't it?'

'Over here, and stop moaning,' yelled Old Edmonds. I

clambered up on to the truck and started handing down jerrycans of water to Shorty and Beachy, who scurried with them to where a depot officer was organizing a stack several yards away.

'There's thousands of gallons of water here,' I said to Beachy, 'surely he'll let us have a can when we've unloaded this little lot.' Drinking water had been so scarce since D-Day that we had resorted to quaffing pints of calvados, the local brew made from apples, to slake our thirst, and for shaving and washing we had been using dirty canal water. Now we were gasping for a drink after being dehydrated by the heat of the fires.

'I'll ask the officer for a can,' said Beachy. As the two passed each other I heard the officer say:

'No, you bloody well can't have a can of water.'

'The stingy bastard – and here's us helping him unload this lot,' I said to my two oppos.

After the truck was unloaded Lieutenant Soulsby ordered us back to our 'slitters' across the canal. From behind a hedge I signalled to Shorty and Beachy to hang back while I pinched a can of water. Nobody seemed to be about so I nonchalantly strolled out and swung a can from the pile on to my shoulder. I was about to join my mates behind the hedge when the dump officer's head appeared over the stack.

'What d'you think you're doing?' he asked, frowning.

'I was just taking a can for me and my mates across the canal. We haven't had a proper drink of anything for three days now.'

'You put it back soldier, and be on your way,' he said curtly. I looked at him face to face for a few seconds.

'No bloody fear,' I finally answered. 'We deserve a drink of water as much as anybody.' And I turned away from him. He ran round the stack of cans and stood in front of me.

'Put that down now,' he said quietly. I could see my two mates watching through the hedgerow and I felt they were testing my courage. Stupidly I took a pace forward to get past the officer. In a flash his revolver was out and pressing against my neck.

'It's up to you soldier. Take it back or I shoot.' I froze.

'OK, OK, but we're bloody desperate for a drink of something.' I put the can back on the pile and the officer kept his .38 in his hand. He looked angrily at me.

'If you think you've got problems, have a look inside the hospital tent. You won't feel so hard done by then. That's where they need this water.'

'Why didn't you say so in the first place sir,' I said, glad of the chance to save face with my mates, and thankful that the officer was not taking the matter any further.

'Bloody hell, Whitey, I thought he was gonna blow your head off,' said Beachy as we moved off.

'So did I,' I answered, 'but I still don't see how one bloody can would have hurt him.'

'Ah well, we might as well die of thirst as anything else,' said Shorty as we stumbled back to our 'slitters'.

One day followed another in similar fashion and it is difficult to place events in strict chronological order after a lapse of many years. We patrolled, cleaned weapons, grabbed a bite and stood to when the enemy was believed to be pushing forward. At odd hours of the day and night we tried to snatch an hour's catnap before being rudely awoken for some urgent detail. Our bodies – and minds – desperately cried out for sleep, deep luxurious sleep, away from the ear-splitting, nerve-shattering noise all around us. So great was our need for rest that we dozed off whenever we stopped moving. The problem was alleviated to some extent when one platoon from each company was sent back over the canal during the day to rest up in some empty houses. It was heavenly stretching out on dry, bare floorboards instead of enduring cramp, pins and needles and other tortures huddled in a tiny, cold, damp 'slitter'.

During our platoon's first visit to these houses I fell into a comatose state as soon as my head hit the makeshift pillow and was quite insensible to the sounds of war outside. Vaguely I became aware of an almighty crash at the front of the house, the thump of heavy boots on the floorboards and another crash at the rear – all in a matter of seconds. I was too tired to open my eyes; after all, noise had become a way of life to me. There followed another crash and heavy footsteps, but this time I heard voices too, so I raised my head to see what was happening. Three black-faced, green-bereted commandos stood in the doorway with menacing Stens.

'Where are the bastards? Which way did they go?' one snarled.

'Who?' I asked, bleary-eyed and semi-conscious.

'Those two Jerries that just came in, you dozy cunt.' I held out my hands in abject bewilderment and the commandos charged on and out of the back door in pursuit. I never did learn whether they caught their quarry. Of the eight or nine of us sleeping in that room only Shorty and I were aware of the Germans invading our privacy. When the others came round they refused to believe our story.

For some days after the landings odd Germans were being flushed out and in fact we bagged one the day after the incident in the empty houses. A Bofors gun sited on the canal bank had powerful binoculars and sometimes we crept forward to observe German infantry across the Orne digging in and generally attending their daily chores. During one of these peekaboo sessions Bertie Bloomfield, a little Cockney, shouted:

'Fack me, chaps, look aht! What's this geezer up to?' Through the glasses we saw a solitary German trooper approaching, waving a piece of brown paper; evidently he could find nothing white to wave. When he eventually reached us he looked very frightened and wanted to give himself up.

'We don't want to be bothered with him,' said Corporal Burke. 'Take him to company HQ, Whitey.' Just then an attractive mademoiselle ran towards us, distraught and tearful, and flung her arms around our prisoner.

'Erich, Erich, oh Erich!' she wailed. We stood nonplussed.

'What a bleedin' carry on,' said Bertie. 'This Froggy bag is asking to get herself done in if the Maquis cop her.'

'What shall I do, Corp?' I asked innocently.

'Take him to company HQ like I told you,' he ordered sharply.

'What about her?' I asked. There were shouts of 'Get off him, you French whore,' '*Allez, allez,*' 'Bugger off, you Froggy tart,' and men shook their guns at her and tried to pull them apart. But it was all to no avail; she clung desperately to her Erich. I looked at Corporal Burke again.

'Oh, for Christ's sake, take the pair of 'em. Let the major sort it out,' he finally said.

The German trooper began crying and his girlfriend's wailing was becoming an embarrassment. Perhaps she thought he was about to be shot. I beckoned to them both and arm in arm they headed for company HQ, located in a house a little way back.

'What's all this?' demanded our sergeant-major. The CSM was a bully and a tyrant, and his attitude was predictable.

'Prisoner, Sarge-Major,' I announced. 'Just given himself up. That's his girlfriend. She won't leave him.'

'Oh she won't, eh? We'll soon see about that.'

I could well guess the CSM's intentions, but I had no desire to loiter and see the German and his lady friend humiliated. I hurried back to the canal, leaving the sergeant-major glaring at the pathetic, blubbering couple. Our CSM would be in his element terrifying them.

One day we received a strange and frightening order: all Bren teams were to report to company HQ with Brens and all the mags they could carry. Shorty and I, laden with equipment, joined our mates from the other two platoons. Three Brens to a platoon meant nine from each company – a total of thirty-six Brens in the battalion, intent on doing something, somewhere. But what? And where? We were mystified as we hurriedly piled into lorries with engines already running and careered down the road. It was a hot, sticky day and clouds of white dust billowed in the convoy's wake. An officer on board spoke to us:

'Jerry's pushing hard and things don't look too good. He's only just up the road.' We screeched to a halt in an orchard and urgent orders began flying in all directions:

'A Brens – follow me.' 'B at the double – this way.' 'Over here, C Brens.' 'D – make it sharp.' We were B Company and our nine teams ran after a beckoning lieutenant. Shorty and I squatted behind a grassy bank while others were placed in hedges and hollows and behind roadside walls. There was no time to dig in, though luckily we were concealed and most of us had some measure of protection. Our lieutenant crawled along the line of Brens with pretty daunting orders:

'Shoot at anything or anyone approaching.'

Thirty-six Brens strung out in line was an impressive array of firepower in the hands of trained, determined squaddies. The Bren, though not as fast as the German Spandau, was an excellent weapon – probably the best light machine-gun ever produced, as British troops in campaigns throughout the world would testify. It was accurate at well over 600 yards, reliable too, and its light weight (just over 20 lb) enabled it to be carried quite easily into battle and if necessary fired from the hip.

For all our firepower we would be useless against the infamous Panzers, which fortunately had so far not shown themselves – at least not in our sector. Only later did we hear that a large proportion of the enemy's mechanized columns were tied up in the Pas de Calais, further north, where Hitler and his generals expected the real invasion. To them we were merely a diversion.

Squatted behind our Bren, with a stack of magazines to hand, Shorty and I stared hard across the field ahead. We heard artillery and machine-gun fire up front, but our immediate vicinity was quiet. In the field were several dead cows, looking grotesque with legs in the air, no doubt victims of the deadly German airbursts, which scattered shrapnel indiscriminately over the whole countryside. The sickly-sweet smell from the corpses, bloated now and festooned with fat maggots, and the fetid odour of soured milk from their ruptured udders seemed to hang heavily on the still, summer air.

We were startled by a big, brawny military police officer who crouched alongside us.

'Orders are – there is to be no Dunkirk this time,' he said in a matter-of-fact tone. 'You must stay here and fight it out. My men are between you and the beaches, with orders to shoot anyone leaving his post. OK?'

'Righto, sir,' we mumbled. The officer crawled along the line, stopping off at each post, presumably to deliver a similar message.

'Bloody hell!' exclaimed Shorty. 'I had no idea things were so bad.'

'Me neither. Let's hope Jerry doesn't send his Panzers in.'

Occasionally an officer joined us, looking very serious as he peered through binoculars, but there was no sign of the enemy, despite continued heavy firing in the distance.

Lying alongside Shorty, waiting for the unknown, I felt scared – all the more so after the redcap's severe warning – but I was not gripped by the all-conquering fear that would assail me later in the campaign. I was still relatively fresh to life at the sharp end and I had the strength of mind to surmount my fears. Allied to this was the fact that morale generally was still high, and beside me, sharing the danger, was my good mate Shorty, who was a calming, reassuring influence. He hailed from Surrey and was only a year or two older than me, but already his dark hair was thinning on top. I had soon discovered that he was brave, with an unruffled disposition; he had strong principles and was just the type to have around if the going got tough. When he smiled his chubby cheeks piled up under his eyes, though he was reluctant to open his mouth in a full grin lest he reveal several missing teeth – the result of numerous brawls.

Later in the afternoon we spotted a khaki-clad figure stumbling along a hedge up ahead. As he drew near we recognized him as one of our former platoon commanders who had transferred to the 17-pounder anti-tank guns attached to the battalion. He looked startled when he saw us.

'Oh, hello you two. I'll have a minute with you. Must get my breath back, y'know.' He dropped down beside us, looking embarrassed and awkward.

'What's happening up there, sir?' Shorty asked him. 'Is it really bad?'

'Oh yes, pretty grim. My three guns have been overrun. Jerry appeared from everywhere. There was no chance to use the radio. I'm just off back to report it and get orders.'

'Be careful when you leave us, sir,' I warned. 'Redcaps have orders to shoot anyone pulling back. Of course it won't apply to you,' I hastily added, 'but you'd better be careful.' The young officer looked thoughtful and swallowed.

'Well, I'll wait here a little longer. I doubt if much can be done now, anyway.' He stayed with us all through that long, hot, sultry afternoon while we maintained a constant vigil. A strange, uncanny silence descended on the foreground, and even the summer birdsong was absent, as though the wildlife too sensed that something was amiss. The oppressive sun beat down mercilessly until the sweat trickled into my eyes and mouth, and still the enemy failed to show. In late afternoon our tanks put in a welcome appearance and began swanning about in nearby woods. This was the signal for our young officer companion to bid us goodbye.

'Thanks for the company,' he said. 'I'll get back to my gunners. They'll have looked after themselves, I know.' He seemed much calmer and more composed than when he joined us earlier. Shorty and I felt that he had panicked and was 'doing a runner' until I mentioned the threatening redcaps.

The solid line of Brens remained in position all through the night and at dawn, when the firing up front had subsided, our officer returned us by Jeep to our canal trenches.

June gave way to July and while events were apparently beginning to move apace elsewhere, we on Sword remained in our constricted beachhead. On night patrols Beachy, Shorty and

I followed the banks of the Orne to its mouth and turned left along the original Sword beach, eerily silent now, save for the dull, rhythmic pounding of the white-frothed rollers that still yielded up an occasional body. We stood on the dunes watching the fearful German V1 rockets, with their throbbing drone, heading towards Blighty. These flying bombs, or doodle-bugs as they were called, and the later V2s, with which Hitler hoped to bring Britain to its knees, caused great anxiety among the squaddies, who feared for their loved ones back home. There was much anger too at the thought of innocent women and children being slaughtered haphazardly. But the terror weapons were to prove a double-edged sword, since they galvanized the lads into a gritty determination to see the job through quickly and in the short term to overrun the rocket launching sites further north. Some of the lads thought we had been outsmarted by the Germans, who would invade England now that our armies had been committed to the Continent.

Unexplained fires continued to break out at the ammunition dumps and in an effort to track down the culprits our platoon was sent over the canal bridge to reconnoitre. After we had combed the area around one large dump, searching hedgerows, an adjacent cornfield and other likely hiding places, Lieutenant Soulsby placed us strategically to watch for approaching intruders. Beachy, Shorty and I set up the Bren on the edge of the cornfield, where we could observe any movement down the flank. It had been a long, gruelling day with no respite and now, as night approached, incessant wind-swept rain lashed us while we huddled among the tall stalks of corn. Despite the atrocious weather we committed the cardinal sin: we fell asleep while on watch.

In a daze I heard voices:

'Old Edmonds reckons they're round here somewhere.' It was the Cockney voice of Corporal Burke. 'Maybe Jerry lifted the buggers in the night.'

'Well, they're not here,' said Banger Brown. 'Let's get back.'

My mind slowly cleared and I realized they were looking for us. But why had we not been spotted? I lifted my head to look around and nearly panicked. We seemed to be buried, though daylight dimly filtered through. Then the truth hit me. We had succumbed to intense fatigue and during the night the wind and rain had battered the corn stalks over us, so that our bodies were enmeshed in wet corn, forming a sort of straw igloo. No wonder Burkey and Banger failed to see us.

I quickly roused my two oppos.

'Bloody hell! Did we fall asleep?' asked Shorty.

'For God's sake don't tell anyone,' said Beachy, slowly coming to. 'Just say we were waiting for someone to fetch us.'

We hurried back over the canal to our platoon HQ.

'Where the hell have you three been?' demanded Old Edmonds.

'We just lay there waiting,' said Beachy, not very convincingly.

'But I sent men after you,' insisted the sergeant. My mates looked at me. To Sergeant Edmonds I was a paragon of virtue.

'We did camouflage up pretty well, Sarge,' I said. 'Sorry if we caused any trouble.'

'Well clean up that Bren – double quick,' ordered Old Edmonds, dismissing us. We were lucky. Had Lieutenant Soulsby looked in on those watch hours we would have been in serious trouble.

Our company sergeant-major – nicknamed the Phantom because he was never around when the going got tough, or when a patrol had to go out – began to show himself a little more now that the situation had eased. He had us fall in and marched us across a rough football pitch near the beach amid much mumbling from the ranks. This was one of our rare quiet moments, and to spend it drilling was ludicrous – especially so near the front line.

'What's the barmy bugger up to?' muttered Beachy. We soon found out.

'Left, right, company to the front salute!' barked the CSM. There was a gasp from the men like a locomotive emitting excess steam. This was 'rookie drill', which recruits practised before being allowed out of the barracks. In protest no one saluted. The Phantom, livid, almost choking, screamed: 'What's the matter with you? To the front salute. To the front salute, I said.' There were angry mutterings among the ranks.

'That bastard's gone too far this time,' said ex-Para Newman, glaring at the Phantom.

Just then several Jeeps loaded with Paras drove slowly by, and their ribald comments and whistles only aggravated an already explosive situation. Good Old Edmonds saved the day by having a few quiet words with the Phantom, after which the other

NCOs relayed the message to us: 'Obey the last order and we'll all go back to proper soldiering.' This time, when the sergeant-major gave the order to salute, arms limply flopped up and flopped down again and we were dismissed. Front line work bares a man's soul, and the Phantom was truly exposed, revealing his bullying, cowardly nature. I never knew what happened to him, but the whole company was glad when he left us.

We continued to be 'stonked' regularly and accurately by enemy artillery across the Orne and all we could do was cower in our 'slitters' and keep our fingers crossed. Major Kaye, crouching behind a fallen tree, was talking to Lieutenant Soulsby.

'We desperately need a good sized doover [a half-covered trench] for our O Groups, away from Jerry's prying eyes, and I think I've found the place. There's a tiny field behind those houses with a tall hedge. Get some of your chaps to sweep it for mines and then construct a good strong doover.'

'Leave it to me sir,' nodded our lieutenant. He only had to turn his head to see Shorty and me in our 'slitter', pretending we were not listening.

'You've done a session with the PMD [Polish Mine Detector] haven't you, Whitehouse?' he said rather than asked. 'Who was with you?'

'Private Beach, sir,' I answered.

'Right. You, Beach and Corporal Smith can tackle that little job.' My heart sank into my boots. Sweeping for mines was a dangerous job, even for the Royal Engineers, and Beachy and I had done a mere two-hour course with dummy mines six months earlier. When I told Beachy that Corporal Smith would accompany us he blew out his cheeks.

'Jesus wept! Smudger!' I knew what he meant. Back in England Corporal Smith was the epitome of an infantry NCO: always immaculate with small pack high on his back and steel helmet at a rakish angle. On manoeuvres he led from the front, yelling and cursing, waving his Tommy gun (which he brandished like a child's pop-gun), and shooting or coshing everyone in sight. I had heard other squaddies say: 'I wish I could get in Smudger's section. He's a useful bloke and would look after you.'

But since landing in Normandy he had been fighting

strenuously to avoid any involvement with the enemy. He camouflaged his 'slitter' so well that even we had difficulty finding it, and it was so deep he had to stand on an ammunition box to see over the top. So desperate was he to get home that at night he rubbed dust into his mosquito bites in the hope of their becoming infected. When Beachy and I reported to him he was annoyed.

'Who the bloody hell put me in for this job?' he moaned. 'I should be in dock. I've got terrible piles and I'm covered in insect bites.' We listened unsympathetically to his whining before Beachy interrupted:

'Well Smudge, to tell the truth I'm just plain shit-scared. How about you, Whitey?'

'How d'you think I feel?' I answered. 'It's me that's doing the bleedin' sweeping. You're OK, Smudger, you've only got to watch.' We collected the mine-sweeping gear and after locating the small patch of rough grass I began sweeping.

I edged forward slowly, moving the detector from side to side, while Beachy followed, skewering the white tape to mark a clear pathway. After about five yards my earphones screeched, bringing me to a sudden halt with the detector head hovering over a suspect mine. With sweat oozing from every pore I moved back, leaving Beachy to probe gingerly with his bayonet, while Smudger watched from a safe distance. Soon Beachy stood up, grinning broadly and holding up a piece of shrapnel. Back along the tape I went and soon the earphones screeched again. This time Beachy bent down, picked up another chunk of shrapnel and threw it at Smudger, shouting 'Bang!' The corporal was not amused. Our antics continued in this way until the area had been cleared of shrapnel, by which time Smudger was gripped by the jitters and ready to collapse.

At dusk Beachy and I returned to begin the officers' doover. The moon was bright, creating an eerie atmosphere, and although the gods of war gravely rumbled all around us, our little patch was deathly silent. Pausing for a breather after strenuous digging, I detected a faint noise on the other side of the nearby hedge and signalled to my mate to be quiet. We listened intently and heard someone walking softly. I pointed my Sten towards the sound, debating whether to challenge and risk being shot or shoot first and ask questions later. The decision was made for me when a dulcet voice wafted through the night:

'*Nous avons café ici pour vous, Tommies.*'

'What's she say?' asked Beachy.

'The lady's brought us coffee,' I chuckled. Luckily my text-book French, learnt in school, had not deserted me.

'*Un moment, mademoiselle,*' I whispered back. I hacked at the hedge with my shovel and made a gap through which, in the moonlight, I saw a pretty little face. The girl was carrying a flask, which she passed to me.

'*Merci, mademoiselle,*' I said with all the fervour I could command. The girl smiled sweetly and walked away towards a lone house whose roof was in a dreadful state, due no doubt to shelling.

During the following days I became very friendly with the maiden, 16-year-old Simone, and would creep out after dark to meet her. She was a lovely, sweet-natured young lady and acted as my contact among the locals, exchanging our tinned pilchards and cigarettes for cheese, butter and eggs, unattainable luxuries to us squaddies. When the bartering was over, like most juveniles we would snatch blissful moments on those dark summer nights to kiss and cuddle. But if my exploring hands strayed into 'forbidden zones' on her vibrant body a torrent of Gallic, followed by a slap across the cheek, soon let me know that she had no intention of being personally liberated by this randy English youth.

After our battalion had left the area Simone and I exchanged letters for a while, but sadly lost touch. However, in 1974, to commemorate the thirtieth anniversary of D-Day, our local paper held a competition for the best story of the event and I entered, writing about the lovely Simone and expressing a desire to meet her again. My story won and the prize was a nostalgic return trip to Normandy, where I had a wonderful reunion with my little mademoiselle. I marvelled at seeing that small field again, just as I had left it thirty years earlier; even the gap I had hacked in the hedge was still discernible. It seemed that time had stood still in that delightful Norman locale.

Corporal Smith, by the way, was soon shipped back to Blighty, but returned to the Continent with another battalion and was blinded by shell blast towards the end of the war.

One night several of us were detailed to construct a camouflaged observation post near the River Orne and thereafter at dusk each day a sniper and two other men went out to man the post until being relieved the following evening. I was sent out with sniper Brummie Robins and Ken Holden from Newton Abbot and we settled down to the standard routine of two hours on and four sleeping. We were connected to platoon HQ by field telephone and had to report any unusual sightings, or the flashes of enemy big guns, which were troubling the beaches. No one had been able to locate these elusive guns, since there was no tell-tale smoke or flash, and we too drew a blank. At dawn, after a quiet night, we drank some self-heating soup to warm our chilled bodies. Suddenly Brummie Robins, using his binoculars, let out a stifled cry.

'Bloody hell,' he said breathlessly, 'look at that.' He slipped the glasses from around his neck, passed them to me and then aimed his rifle and adjusted the sniper lens. Peering through the glasses I saw the heads and shoulders of three Germans, who must have been lying on a small embankment on the far side of the river. Two were peering through binoculars and the third was casting glances all around him. I passed the glasses to Ken and while he was viewing the scene I steadied my rifle on a beam that formed part of our 'window'.

'Stan, you and me both aim at the Jerry in the middle,' murmured Brummie. I had already noticed this German was wearing quite an imposing hat decked in braid and laurel leaves.

'Ken, you take the other one with the binocs,' continued our sniper. 'Got 'em?' We both grunted assent.

'On three then,' said Brummie quietly. 'One, two, three.' The three rifles went off as one.

'Right, let's get out fast now,' Brummie ordered. But first he cranked the field phone and warned our forward positions that we would be coming in, since we were not due back until dusk. Lieutenant Soulsby was on hand to ensure that our lads did not shoot us up, and to hear our story, which we let Brummie relate. He gave a colourful description of the whole incident with emphasis on the German with the decorative hat.

'Do you think you hit him?' asked the lieutenant, delighted at being able to report the news to his superiors.

'I'm bloody sure I did,' said Brummie Robins emphatically.

'How about you two?' The officer looked at Ken and me.

'Yeah, suppose we must have,' we agreed. As we finished speaking explosions came from the riverside we had just left and continued for about ten minutes.

'That's why we got out fast,' said our sniper mate. 'Once you've made a killing it pays to scarper. They'll be watching that river bank for days now.'

'That was bloody exciting, Ken,' I said to my mate a little later.

'Yeah,' he agreed with a wry smile. 'I reckon they should ship you home when you've shot a Jerry and send some other bugger out to shoot one. That way we'll soon get rid of 'em.'

The German artillery across the Orne continued to fox our officers, who were desperate to pinpoint their position. I had become friendly with a likeable Norman youth about my age who pestered me to have him sent to England, where he hoped to join our navy. During our chats I mentioned, in my halting French, the mystery of these big guns, whereupon he became very excited, assuring me that he had been forced to work on the guns, which apparently had an attachment for eliminating the flash and smoke. I took the lad to Lieutenant Soulsby who soon had him at company HQ poring over maps and pinpointing the exact location of the troublesome artillery. The guns were eventually eliminated, though I never heard whether the young Frenchman managed to join our navy.

One night our company was dug in alongside a spinney bordering the canal. We were alert for enemy infiltrators, but had to be heedful of Red Berets, still drifting back over the canal in small groups. To complicate matters it was reported that German commandos intended coming down the Orne by raft or mini-sub to raid the beachhead.

I was teamed up with my mate Shorty and from our cramped 'slitter' we heard rustling in the nearby bushes. We were reluctant to open fire for fear of hitting returning Paras or giving our position away.

'I'll use a phosphor grenade,' whispered Shorty. 'It'll set fire to the scrub and we can see who's there.' I nodded agreement. Now the phosphorus bomb was a complicated, temperamental device operated by removing a cap and unwinding a tape which released the pin and it had to be treated with the utmost respect. Shorty threw the bomb and let out a muffled cry.

'Christ, the damned thing slipped. Duck!' We crouched low but nothing happened. Peering over the rim of our trench we saw that all was quiet. At dawn, after an uneventful night, we reported the incident of the unexploded bomb to Lieutenant Soulsby when he did his rounds.

'It's too dangerous lying there,' said the lieutenant. 'I'll go forward for it when the light improves.' True to his word he returned later and found the bomb lying about fifteen feet from our 'slitter'.

'I'll see if it will activate by hitting it with stones,' he said. 'Collect some large stones and then retire to those trees further back.'

By this time the whole platoon knew what was afoot and sheltered behind the trees to watch the proceedings. Standing in our 'slitter' the lieutenant began hurling the stones, hoping that one would jar the pin out and explode the device. From behind the trees various instructions were being quietly called out:

'Up a bit,' 'Not so far,' 'Left a bit,' and so on. Becoming frustrated at his lack of success, especially in front of his whole platoon, and seeing the pile of stones dwindling fast, the lieutenant left the trench, took several paces forward, and threw a particularly large stone. A loud whoosh! followed and a fountain of glowing embers cascaded over him.

'Bloody hell! Help me,' he screamed, dashing about in circles and tearing at his smouldering clothes, as though he were being chased by a swarm of angry bees. In the panic his tin hat fell off and phosphorus began singeing his hair, while little puffs of smoke emanated from his battle-dress. We managed to dive on him to help remove his burning clothes, but he knocked us over in his futile efforts to escape the phosphorus penetrating to his skin.

'Cut his trousers off with your jack knives,' yelled Old Edmonds, who had appeared on the scene. Half a dozen jack knives flashed open.

'No, no, roll me in the grass,' shouted the lieutenant, horrified at the sight of the knives being brandished. His face and hands were pock-marked with little yellow-edged holes, and when we ripped off his blouse and shirt his chest and back were similarly affected.

'Look out! Stand back!' he finally called and dashed headlong for the nearby canal. Stripped to the waist and with tattered trousers trailing behind, he looked a strange sight rushing pell-mell through the spinney. There was a great splash and the lieutenant bellyflopped into the canal. Someone swore he heard a loud hissing noise as our platoon leader submerged. When he surfaced the medics wrapped him in a blanket and drove him to the RAP (Regimental Aid Post). Sadly we never saw Lieutenant Soulsby again. At the time the incident looked comical, almost farcical, and was accentuated by the officer's prominent front teeth and protruding behind – a caricaturist's dream. But he was badly burned and I can only assume that he was invalided home. In the coming months we were to have a succession of replacement platoon leaders, but none could match the first. He was a wonderful, courageous, caring officer who led by example, and he was greatly missed.

One outcome of this incident was that those of us still carrying phosphorus bombs discreetly 'lost' them in double quick time. The thought of one being hit by shrapnel while in its breast ammunition pouch was too horrific to contemplate.

In mid-July we received news that saddened us. The battalion was being split up to reinforce the assault groups, who had suffered heavy casualties since D-Day. We were given the option of joining the Paras, the Commandos, the Black Watch or the Argylls, and I chose the Black Watch, along with the majority of our lads. We were badly needed at the sharp end for a break-out, which did not augur well.

3   With the Black Watch

The 1st Battalion Black Watch HQ was located a couple of miles up the road in a farmstead, and we waited in their B echelon field while our officers reported in. I noticed squaddies nearby laying out 'big packs' and counted sixty-four, arranged in neat rows. (No infantry go into action wearing 'big packs', which follow behind with B echelon.) As there were sixty-four of us I assumed they were ours.

'That was quick,' I said, turning to Shorty, 'they've brought up our big 'uns already.'

'Good,' he said. 'I could do with something from mine. I'll nip over for it.' He ambled towards a squaddie carrying a clipboard, exchanged a few words and returned.

'No joy?' asked Beachy. Shorty sighed.

'No, the packs belong to the lads we're replacing. They were all killed in the last few days. They're sorting out personal items to send home for next of kin.'

Sixty-four packs, sixty-four of us. I felt my stomach go taut and the hairs on the back of my neck seemed to rise. Once again the seeds of fear were being sown. I was glad when the QM ordered us to throw our berets into one tea-chest and choose a tam o' shanter that fitted from another. I liked the Watch's distinctive soft hat, with its red hackle or feather, but the enemy's frequent shelling and mortaring decreed that tin hats were the fashion of the day.

I was to learn later that the Black Watch had a long and meritorious history, dating back to 1725 when independent companies were formed in the Scottish Highlands to keep watch and maintain peace among feuding clans. They were known as the Highland Watch, and when they adopted a dark tartan uniform the name Black Watch was born. They fought with distinction at Waterloo, in the Crimea, during the Boer War and in most of the major First World War battles.

In 1939 the 1st Battalion went to France as part of the BEF, but following the German breakthrough in 1940 they were trapped at St Valery on the French coast and forced to surrender after running out of food and ammunition. Only a handful of men evaded capture or escaped. In 1942 the rebuilt 1st Battalion, as members of the 51st Highland Division, went to the Middle East, where they distinguished themselves at El Alamein and in Sicily, after which they returned home to prepare for the Normandy landings. With the 7th Battalion Black Watch and the 7th Argyll and Sutherland Highlanders, we now comprised 154 Brigade, and I felt proud to be a member of the famous 51st Highland Division.

Luckily the old Bucks Battalion platoon that had been together for more than two years remained virtually intact, which was a tremendous fillip. The companionship of staunch mates like Shorty and Beachy and Old Edmonds made life a little more tolerable. Then there was Ray Cheadle, another good pal; Johnny Newman, thrown out of the Paras for being undisciplined; Corporal Fitzsimmons (Fitz), who became a sergeant; and Eddie Head, a scallywag and the scruffiest soldier I ever saw, but fearless. They were all trusty mates who could be relied on when we were in a tight spot.

A platoon is like a large family of about forty men, living and eating and sleeping together for month after month. They laugh and cry over shared experiences, get drunk together and fight the common enemy. Is it any wonder then that such powerful bonds are forged between them, bonds stronger even than those between blood brothers? Truly they are ready to die for each other – and sometimes do – and when a member of the 'family' is killed or maimed the rest feel a deep anguish and express a blinding hatred for the perpetrators.

We were now number 6 Platoon in B Company and moved up to the front that night to dig in alongside our new buddies and were immediately greeted by a heavy artillery barrage from German 88s. It was as though the enemy sensed our arrival and were welcoming us to the front line.

After an O Group the next morning our officer informed us that we were to take a hill just ahead, which was obscured by heavy mist. There would be no preceding barrage, which was unusual, but it was hoped that the mist would cloak our movements. As we formed up I sensed a bad feeling among the old Watch lads. Apparently our stretcher-bearers had been shot up the previous day while retrieving wounded comrades. Although some of the enemy – particularly the SS – had shown themselves to be ruthless and cold-blooded, there was an unwritten law among the infantry on both sides that men tending the wounded would be unmolested. Any side breaking that law was wide open for retribution. I was to discover that this rancour between the Watch and the Germans would persist to the bitter end. During most actions there seemed to be 'incidents', but whether these were coincidental or old scores being settled it was difficult to say. Nevertheless, I came to the conclusion that the Watch had a bad reputation in German eyes, though I was unaware of any conduct (or misconduct) that would warrant such a reputation.

With the countryside still wrapped in mist we moved off to attack the hill, and despite the chilly morning I sweated profusely. It was a tremendous relief to find the German positions unoccupied, with signs of a hasty retreat, including hot food tins left near fox-holes. Our quiet approach had worked; to the enemy we must have looked like wraiths emerging through the mist.

Apparently the Norman town of Caen, an important road and rail junction, should have been taken on D-Day, according to Allied forecasts, but weeks after the landings it remained firmly in enemy hands. The town had now been turned into a formidable stronghold and was becoming a festering sore to our top brass. Although we were unaware of it at the time, General Montgomery and the British army in general were accused of being over-cautious and dilatory by many people, who thought that by now we should be at the gates of Paris, or at least well clear of the original bridgehead. Had our critics joined us in facing the cream of the German army – including the infamous SS – their carping might have been more restrained. For now the whole British and Canadian front was bogged down as the enemy massed their armour and artillery around Caen.

Earlier we had witnessed the bombing of the town by hundreds of Lancasters. First a number of low-flying planes – evidently pathfinders – cruised around, marking the target. Then the main body sailed majestically over, keeping good station, despite heavy flak. It was an awe-inspiring, uplifting sight that did our morale a power of good. A number of planes were hit though, and we counted the parachutes as they billowed out, some airmen luckily landing near our own lines, from where they were rescued by scout cars dashing in.

Now, as part of the 51st Highland Division, we became indirectly involved in the battle for Caen. The country up ahead, with its broad, rolling plains, was more open, and to cross on foot would have invited heavy casualties. We therefore travelled in Kangaroos, which were tanks with the turrets removed, allowing each to carry seven or eight men and giving some measure of protection. It was a nightmare eight-hour journey as we cowered down while shrapnel and bullets pinged off the armoured vehicle's sides. We had to pee in our empty food tins and throw the contents over the side. I did notice quite a number of dead Germans lying along our route, and a Kangaroo just ahead was hit, whereupon the squaddies aboard baled out, only to disappear in two simultaneous explosions of dirt and smoke.

That long, hair-raising Kangaroo ride finally ended as darkness fell, when we had detoured Caen, and were able to stretch our stiff, aching legs before digging in.

The ordeal of running the gauntlet to get around Caen left us badly shaken, and while most of us soon recovered, one or two were left in a pathetic state. In particular Mushty, a young lad from Cornwall, began crying and sobbing to anyone prepared to listen, fervently hoping that he would be sent back. He was a pitiable sight as he sidled up to squaddies, bemoaning his fate, all the while trembling uncontrollably. Our officer had sternly told us newcomers to the regiment, 'There is no such thing as "bomb happiness" [battle fatigue or shell shock] in the Black Watch.' When Mushty had calmed down a little he approached me.

'Bugger it Whitey, I'm shagged,' he said despairingly, 'but I'll keep going and if God wants me He'll have to take me, and if He doesn't – well, I'll get through.' He strolled about the front area in an upright posture, quite oblivious to the danger of flying shrapnel and bullets. This became known as the 'deathwish walk', as opposed to the infantry crouch we had all instinctively adopted very early on. To a stranger Mushty would have seemed casual, even brave, nonchalantly sauntering around the 'sharp end', but a closer examination of his face would have revealed a gaunt expression and real fear in his eyes. He was praying that something – bullet or shell – would put him out of his misery.

I found the French peasants and farmers generally friendly and glad to see us, although I later heard that in other sectors they were rude, discourteous, and even hostile towards our lads. I suppose this attitude was understandable after we had wrecked their houses and farm buildings, ruined crops and killed countless livestock. Some locals thought that our presence in Normandy was merely a Dieppe-type hit-and-run raid, and that once we had returned to England they would reap the consequences from their oppressors.

After my bartering prowess with Simone, and because of my knowledge of the language, I was appointed our platoon's negotiator among the locals, who would trade almost anything for our cigarettes. These reached us in the fourteen-man compo packs, which also included treacle puddings, sweets, triangular sausages, soups and toilet paper. But there was a near mutiny among the front-liners when we discovered that compo boxes were being cut open *en route* and the precious cigarettes rifled. The lorry drivers blamed the stores personnel and the base wallahs blamed the drivers.

As the weather improved flies and mosquitoes became more than just a nuisance. While up front I was bitten so badly about the face that I had to stop shaving after slicing the tops off the half-healed bites. The sergeant-major saw my stubble and reported me to the company commander, who gave me three days 'spud-bashing' when the Argylls passed through us and we were placed in reserve.

We hated night attacks, especially in the early Normandy days, when it was all so strange to us. During daylight forays we could at least rely on visual contact to keep in touch, but after dark units often became confused and disorientated, particularly if tall hedges intervened, rendering our poor quality radios almost useless.

Our company (B) were digging in after one night sortie when Lieutenant Yates, our platoon commander, asked for a runner to contact A Company. My sense of direction was dreadful at the best of times, but luckily for me on this moonless night the task fell to my pal Shorty.

He set out in search of A Company and a few minutes later we heard a sustained burst of Sten fire, followed by complete silence. On tenterhooks, we faced the direction of the firing and soon heard someone crashing through the undergrowth. Then a hushed voice called out:

'Shorty here, where are you Black Watch?'

'Over here,' someone whispered and Shorty emerged from the darkness and collapsed among us.

'Thank Christ for that,' gasped my mate, his chest heaving like a bellows as he gulped great draughts of air.

'What happened?' asked Sergeant Edmonds. 'Did our boys fire on you?' That was always a big danger for runners at night. Shorty was still panting heavily, but eventually managed to relate his story.

'Soon after leaving here I heard voices, and as every other word seemed to end in 'och' or 'uch' or 'ich' I assumed they were the Jocks of A Company. I still can't get used to their lingo. Not wantin' to scare 'em, I crept up quietly and saw they were bent down digging a trench, with no helmets on. There were three of 'em that I could make out. I was within a couple of feet when I saw the uniforms. Bloody hell! They were Jerries! I would have backed off but one spotted me and I had to open fire. That was too bloody close for me.'

We all listened enthralled and praised Shorty for his stirring deeds.

'Did you get to A Company, Shorthouse?' asked the practical Sergeant Edmonds.

'Did I buggery, Sarge. I was lucky to get back here.'

'All right, all right,' said the lieutenant, who had been listening with the rest of us. 'Everybody keep alert. We'll investigate in the morning.'

The following morning we had a visit from Major Anderson, our popular company commander, the RSM and their retinue.

'What was that shooting in front of your positions last night?' the major asked Lieutenant Yates.

'We were just about to go and see, sir,' answered the lieutenant. 'I sent Shorthouse here to contact A Company and he had a brush with some Jerries.'

'Right, let's go and see what happened,' said the major. 'Lead on,' he signalled to Shorty.

Sure enough they found three dead Germans, all riddled

from the waist up, slumped in their half-finished trench. They had been a Spandau team, probably as lost as we all seemed to be that dark night. Shorty's prompt action in silencing the machine-gun had undoubtedly saved lives and earned him a well-deserved Military Medal.

The wet, cold, miserable days of June had given way to glorious July weather when our platoon led an advance deep in the Norman *bocage* country, with its complexity of fields and hedges. These small fields, surrounded by six-foot-high banks topped with dense hedges, stretched for miles – ideal terrain for tenacious defenders, as the Germans had proved to be, but difficult for our tanks to manoeuvre in.

I felt naked advancing in this hinterland, where I imagined every hedge and every narrow, twisting lane hid a Spandau or a Panzerfaust – the German bazooka. Not surprisingly progress was slow – too slow for the tanks accompanying us. A tank officer leaned out of his turret and called to Lieutenant Yates, walking near me:

'Why the hell don't you get a move on? We'll be here all day at this rate.' He was obviously irritated and I detected a touch of sarcasm in his voice. The lieutenant was equal to the occasion.

'I suggest you press on if you're happy there's nobody out there. We are bloody walking, y'know.'

'These tanks are valuable,' snapped the tank officer. 'You push on and make sure there are no bazookas up front. That's the usual drill and you know it.' Our lieutenant bit his tongue. The tank officer was a captain and outranked him.

'OK lads,' he said, 'let's give it a go. Follow me.' And so saying he increased his pace. We had not travelled far when our scout, twenty-five yards ahead, shouted:

'Enemy front,' and opened fire with his Sten. I hit the ground, panting fiercely as sweat – more from fear than the heat – ran into my eyes and down my cheeks into the corners of my mouth until I could taste the salt. The scout scurried back to Lieutenant Yates.

'There they are sir, waiting,' he said excitedly, pointing to the hedge. Three German helmets were just visible over the top of it. The tank officer reappeared and from his turret viewed the hedge through binoculars.

'Something strange there,' he said after a long, hard look.

'They're not moving.' Our lieutenant was also closely scrutinizing the scene through his glasses and realizing something would have to be done quickly he ran forward, ducking and weaving, and disappeared behind the hedge. He emerged grinning and holding a coal-scuttle helmet aloft in each hand.

'Three Jerry graves,' he called out. 'SS men. Come on chaps, move a bit quicker.' A beautifully made cross had been planted at the head of each grave and the helmets placed on top, facing our advance, though we had no way of knowing whether this was a deliberate ploy.

I had to admire Lieutenant Yates, who had taken us under his wing after the loss of Lieutenant Soulsby. He was the archetypal British subaltern: tall, slim, smartly dressed and dashing, the public schoolboy type, right down to his Errol Flynn pencil moustache. When enemy snipers had been a menace earlier in the campaign he was very reluctant to hide his map case, Sam Browne belt and other adornments of authority. He seemed fearless and always remained cool, however tight the situation.

The sight of our lieutenant holding those helmets eased the tension somewhat, though the prospect of an SS unit facing us sent a shiver through me. Throughout all our units, and certainly among the Canadians, the SS had a reputation for being barbaric and cold-hearted.

Because of the dense thickets and narrow, winding byways, which were veritable tank traps in themselves, our armour deserted us to find an easier route and we were left on our own. We pushed forward slowly, painstakingly, through the thick, almost impenetrable growth and began clearing a more open sector of scrubland when it happened. A Spandau opened up with its unmistakable purr – like cloth being torn – and our lead section was chopped down. I hugged the ground closely as the cries of the wounded rang in my ears.

'Stretcher-bearers,' someone shouted.

'Come on you chaps,' said Lieutenant Yates, crawling up to our section. 'Let's get up there and help them. Follow me.' He led us off at an angle away from our wounded mates, into denser scrub, and then swung towards the stricken section, actually coming out ahead of them. Two were dead, three wounded, and the other two seemed all right, just too terrified to speak or move. I had seen this happen before. The sudden shock and the sight of dead and wounded mates could render lads completely immobile and speechless.

'Whitehouse, go back and guide the stretcher lads through the way we came,' ordered our lieutenant, as cool as ice. But Corporal Tom King and his stretcher boys, old hands at the game, had already found the safe way through. I helped to stretcher our wounded to a Red Cross Jeep in a lane some way back and had the jitters as we ran, crouched low, with our heavy loads, expecting the Spandau to cut us down in our tracks. As the Jeep headed for the RAP I asked Corporal King:

'What about the two dead lads up front?'

'They'll no' be wandering aboot. We'll pick 'em up later,' answered our stretcher-bearer supreme.

By now the whole company was held up by the hidden Spandau, whose short bursts were no help in locating it. Our company commander came among us and spoke to Lieutenant Yates.

'I'm getting a right rollocking from the CO,' I heard him say. 'Where is the bastard?' No sooner had he finished speaking than the enemy machine-gun fired again.

'There sir, over there sir,' someone shouted, pointing to a tangle of logs and fallen trees about 250 yards away.

'Right, my man, you've had your chips,' said the company commander quietly as he verified the position through his glasses. 'I'll contact the three-inch mortars and when they've finished take your chaps in quickly, Yates. We're running well behind time, y'know.'

'Right sir,' the lieutenant nodded.

An old wag overhearing the conversation looked around at us, a bemused expression on his face.

'Running well behind time,' he said softly. 'Running well behind time. That's a bleedin' laugh. What's he think we're on? A bloody chara trip to Blackpool?'

The mortars crashed down on the strongpoint and we advanced, only to be checked by another Spandau burst. Ironically our sole casualty was the old wag, shot in the knee. He was in severe pain, but could console himself with having received a Blighty wound, and not a few of us would have swopped 'the pain for the gain'.

Another mortar salvo straddled the logs and then, led by our platoon commander, we rushed forward, blazing away. We were surprised to find not just a few logs, but a solid, well constructed fortification of interwoven logs, with diggings and a tunnel for a quick exit. Two SS men were spreadeagled on the ground, one dead, but the other merely dazed. Sergeant Edmonds slapped his face roughly and tipped the German's water-bottle over his head.

'Come on, yer Jerry bastard,' he shouted. 'On yer feet.' The SS man slowly came to and struggled upright.

'We haven't the time to question him,' said Lieutenant Yates. 'Send him back to battalion HQ.' Little Wally Walters, eavesdropping, volunteered to escort the prisoner, no doubt hoping for a brief respite from front line duty. Wally was a good little chap, but I suspected he was beginning to crack up, and several times I had noticed his eyes puffy and red as though from weeping. However, it was only a short distance to battalion HQ.

'OK Walters,' said Sergeant Edmonds. 'Got one up the spout?' Wally nodded.

'Right. Keep him three or four yards in front, and if he so much as farts – shoot the bugger.'

'OK Fritz – march!' ordered Wally, motioning the SS man forward with his rifle. We all grinned at little Wally, looking very businesslike as he strode forward.

'*Hände hoch, Hände hoch*, yer bastard,' he shouted, and then disappeared with his charge behind a clump of shrubs.

It was dusk before we reached our designated positions and began digging in like frantic ferrets in case the enemy sent over their dreaded 88s. The German 88mm gun, one of the best of its kind on either side during the war, was originally designed to be used against aircraft, but it proved highly effective as an anti-tank weapon, firing AP shells, and was just as deadly using HE in air bursts against infantry concentrations. Truly, an all-purpose gun.

Relaxing uneasily in my 'slitter' – up front it was impossible to unwind completely – a chill moved through my body, I began sweating heavily and the sweat turned icy cold. It was becoming increasingly difficult now to shake off the effects of each day's traumas, which earlier my powers of resilience had allowed me to overcome. And after a long, gruelling day, with nothing to eat, my spirits were at their lowest and I fell prey to the worst aspects of fear, which was beginning to prove a more formidable foe than the Germans. I felt that if I could conquer this fear my own personal battle would be half won. During the day I was too busy protecting life and limb to dwell on morbid thoughts, but now, crouched below ground, I reflected on our two lads lying dead back there and the others horribly maimed. An occasional spasm of trembling ran through my limbs and I wondered when my number would be up too.

'Grub up!' The whispered call chased away my depression.

'You go first,' I said to Chris Bateman, my 'slitter' oppo, our radio man who hailed from Bristol. He returned ten minutes later.

'Guess what, Whitey,' he gasped.

'The war's over,' I teased.

'No. That SS bastard killed Wally and escaped.' I felt as though crushed ice was slithering all over me.

'Oh no, for Christ's sake, no,' I groaned. 'Are you sure, Batey?'

'Yeah. The cooks found his body when they brought our grub up. He'd been strangled.'

I fetched my rations and while eating tried to imagine the scenario. I could picture little Wally getting over-confident. That three- or four-yard gap would slowly, imperceptibly dwindle, a quick swing round by the German, knocking the rifle aside, would be followed by a vicious kick to send Wally to the ground, and it would be all over for our little mate. Those SS men were professionals all right, and ruthless with it, many having served on the Russian front, where, we had heard, no quarter was given. In contrast the average squaddie would be unable to kill in such a cold-blooded manner.

After breaking the news of Wally's death Batey disappeared for a pee and on jumping back into the trench in the dark let out a yell and clutched his face. I was puzzled at first and unable to answer other lads calling out to enquire if we were all right. It transpired that Batey had left the radio set on the floor of our trench and as he jumped back in the extended aerial pierced his eye. Luckily the cooks were still with us and took him back for urgent treatment. I never saw him again and wondered how he fared. He was another good mate and at one time we became almost inseparable, simply because I was his 'minder'.

As we stalked down Norman lanes Batey always stayed just behind the platoon commander with his earphones on, ready to pick up radio messages. But when we were shelled or mortared he was unable to hear the tell-tale whines and often continued advancing while the rest of us crouched in a roadside ditch. He complained loudly to all who would listen and when something thudded off his helmet while the rest of us lay flat on our bellies, his invective was unfit for chaste ears. Eventually we agreed that I should walk just behind him and on hearing the whine or screech of anything unfriendly approaching I would slap his pack hard. It worked quite well, except when occasionally, in my haste to 'hit the dirt', I forgot to warn my mate. Then he would say nothing, but his scornful look as I sheepishly got to my feet was far more effective than mere curses.

A lone farmstead across fields was assumed to hold the enemy and we were ordered to take it. We moved off at 0400 hours, when darkness and dawn were still trying to sort themselves out, and to complicate matters a heavy mist enveloped the whole countryside. As we cautiously advanced I was amazed to see a man flitting towards us through the mist.

'Welcome Tommy. Drink? Calvados, very good for you.' He darted to each of us, like a bee visiting flowers, and offered a bottle. I took a swig but the squaddie next to me waved him away.

'Bugger off!' he said. 'Where's Jerry?'

The Frenchman came back to me and I took another gulp. It was wonderful, potent stuff, this distilled apple juice.

'Good, Tommy, eh?' he said. 'Bosche gone, Tommy.'

'He says Jerry's gone,' I called out to Sergeant Edmonds, slightly ahead of me and beckoning impatiently for the bottle. Just then enemy automatic fire opened up and we flattened. After a pause Old Edmonds shot up and ran across a smooth piece of ground.

'Jesus bloody wept!' he cursed as he disappeared through the mist. We fired in the general direction of the farmhouse and crept forward. Out of the building, by now just visible, emerged a small group of Germans, with hands held high. I was elated at the sight of these, our first prisoners. One seemed very young, maybe fifteen or sixteen, and he was cocky with it.

'*Haben sie Zigaretten*, Tommy?' he asked. Johnny Newman, the big, brawny ex-Para, kicked him in the behind.

'Stick that in yer pipe and smoke it, yer cheeky little bastard!' he said.

The Germans were searched for watches and other valuables and pushed to the rear. I never took part in this looting of prisoners, deeming it pretty degrading, unless those being filched were SS men, then I frisked them for pistols, knives and watches.

With the farmhouse cleared we were ordered to lie low at a crossroads and await orders. Soon Lieutenant Yates and his batman appeared.

'Where's Sergeant Edmonds?' the officer asked. I had last seen Old Edmonds disappearing into the mist, swearing profusely. Before anyone could stop him, one of the newer lads shouted:

'Sergeant Edmonds. Where are you, Sergeant Edmonds?' After a brief pause came the reply:

'I'm over here chaps – over here.' The voice spoke good English, but it was not Percy Edmonds' distinctive Buckinghamshire brogue. And it came from an area we had not yet cleared.

'Crafty bastards,' muttered our lieutenant. 'Chuck a couple of grenades down there,' he ordered. A squelching sound came from behind us, accompanied by a foul smell. It was Sergeant Edmonds. Apparently in running forward he had fallen into a stagnant, moss-covered pond, which through the mist looked like pastureland.

'Who the bloody hell keeps calling my name out?' he asked angrily. 'Oh, it's you sir, is it?' he said, spotting Lieutenant Yates.

'No, it isn't me. It's a Jerry down there,' replied the officer. As if to corroborate the statement the voice floated again through the mist:

'I'm over here. Where are you?' Old Edmonds was livid. I stood near him holding two grenades I had taken from my pouch earlier.

'Gimme one of those,' he snarled, snatching a grenade. 'Come with me, young 'un.' We followed a hedgerow for some distance, halted and pulled the pins.

'One – two – three – go!' shouted the sergeant, and we hurled the grenades. The NCO's anger seemed to give him added strength and his bomb carried much further than mine. After the explosions a groaning came from where we had earlier heard the voice.

'Take no bloody notice,' said Old Edmonds, who was still seething. 'It's probably another trick.'

'Get back to B echelon for a fresh rig-out, Sergeant,' said our officer, grimacing as the putrid-smelling Old Edmonds and I returned. The sergeant glared in the direction of the continuing groaning and then looked at me:

'Nobody's to go out there. Is that clear?' He obviously thought it was not cricket to play such devious tricks.

Our Bren carriers arrived to strengthen the position and bring up our Benghazi cookers to enable us to make a much-needed 'brew'. As the name implies, the cooker originated in the Western Desert and was merely a large biscuit tin filled with petrol-soaked sand. When lit it gave off intense heat, burned for hours, and, most important, it was smokeless. I relished this part of the routine after an attack when we could relax just a little and stretch our legs.

'I'm off over there for a pony and trap if anyone wants me,' Corporal Burke, the Cockney, said quietly, pointing to a bush that was technically in no man's land. I watched him head for the bush, fiddle with his belt, and then disappear as he crouched low. Suddenly he stood up.

'For fack's sake someone bring me Sten. Get over here – quick,' he yelled. A gigantic German, looking sinister wrapped in his groundsheet-cum-cape, stood before him swaying, hands held high.

'*Kamarad*, Tommy,' he said. '*Kamarad. Ich Ruski*, Tommy. *Ruski*.' The corporal stepped from the bush with one hand clasping his trousers at the knees and the other pointing a threatening finger at the German as if to say Don't you come near me, mate. This hilarious tableau, with the priceless expression on Burkey's face contrasting with the German's dumb, nonplussed look, had us all helpless with laughter.

The German – or rather the Russian – was mumbling and making strange signs which we eventually interpreted as meaning that he wanted help for his mate, still groaning spasmodically after Old Edmonds and I had thrown the grenades. Corporal Tyas (Texas to the lads) and some of us went out with the Bren carrier's stretcher and recovered the badly wounded Russian, who had a ghastly pallor and was probably dying.

Sergeant Edmonds appeared, looking for the Bren carrier to take him back.

'I thought I said not to go out there,' he roared. But when we related the story of Burkey's interrupted ablutions our sergeant almost choked with laughter and his false teeth shot out.

'Poor buggers, they're Russians y'know, Sarge,' said one lad as the stretcher bearing the wounded man passed us.

'Poor buggers my arse,' exploded Old Edmonds, no longer laughing. 'They're firing fuckin' German bullets ain't they?'

Our lines were more fluid now and there were indications that the enemy, hard-pressed on all sides, were beginning to crack. The glorious weather of these July and August days, with their cloudless skies, had enabled our fighter-bombers to be up from dawn, mercilessly strafing German positions almost round the clock.

The gentle countryside hereabouts, with its cider-apple orchards and stone farmhouses was reminiscent of our own West Country, though poplar-lined roads and signposts bearing long, unpronounceable French place-names shattered the illusion.

Our platoon took an isolated farmhouse, and its small garrison, looking tired and drawn, seemed eager to quit. After digging in around the perimeter, I returned to the house to help Sergeant Edmonds prepare bully beef stew. Private Eddie Coombes came in with the farmer, a bronzed, wizened old man with drooping shoulders.

'Hey, Whitey,' said Eddie, 'you know a bit of the lingo, what the bloody hell's this old Froggy on about?' It seemed that the old man, realizing that we were staying, had emerged from his hiding-place. Tears were rolling down his cheeks as he gabbled on in an almost incomprehensible dialect. I managed to pick out odd words and phrases that he repeated.

'A good boy, Tommy ... German, but a good boy ... he is dead ... the SS are pigs.' Then, taking my arm, he led me to a tree at the side of the house and I noticed a rope hanging from one of its stout branches. Prattling on, with the tears still coursing down his weather-beaten cheeks, the farmer pointed to the rope and a little mound of freshly-dug soil near the tree. On top of the mound was a small wooden cross bearing several illegible scribbled words.

With patience and not a little questioning I was eventually able to piece together the sad tale of the little mound. Some days earlier a young German soldier, unable to stand the incessant bombing and shelling any longer, had called at the farm and begged the old man to hide him. When the German rearguard of SS men fell back to the house some days later they found the young deserter and hanged him from the tree. After they had left, the old man cut him down and buried him in the shallow, temporary grave. He was distraught while relating the story, and it was obvious that he had become fond of the youth during their few days together.

Regrettably we could do nothing to console the old man. Later Sergeant Edmonds, practical man that he was, thrust a basin of stew into his gnarled hands.

'Here y'are, old cock,' he said. 'Get this down yer. And think yerself bloody lucky they didn't string you up for harbouring a deserter.' I decided not to translate for the old man.

'Banger' Brown was a clown, always behaving as though he were on the stage. Not much older than me – maybe nineteen – he was tall, with a fine physique. He was happiest making others laugh, but that changed dramatically after we landed in Normandy. Banger had been given his nickname before he joined us, and now there was something ironic about it. Every bang, however distant, turned him into a shaking, morose shadow of the jovial joker we all liked. Fear had eaten into his very vitals, like some malignant disease, affecting his whole outlook. I tried repeatedly to convince him that every shell and bullet was not meant for him personally.

'I'm shit-scared, Whitey,' he would say. 'I don't know why, but I am, and I don't care who knows it, or what they think. I'm a coward – I admit it.'

It was no surprise to us when, just before one sortie, word went round that Banger had gone 'on the trot'. He had taken off in the night with Jock Jarman from another platoon. They were our first 'trotters' and the only surprise was that no one had gone sooner. After weeks of enduring heavy shelling and mortaring, enemy attacks and patrols and occasional Luftwaffe raids, combined with cold, wet nights in our cramped 'slitters', a lack of sleep and slapdash, hurried, usually cold meals, even the toughest among us were showing frayed nerves.

Later we were dug in among apple trees near a farm when our regimental police Jeep swung into the farm and screeched to a stop. In it sat Banger and Jock, looking thoroughly miserable.

'Out, you yellow bastards,' shouted the military police sergeant, pulling hard on Banger's collar. In their effort to move quickly the two squaddies fell out on to the ground in a heap.

'On yer feet, you yellow-livered scum,' the sergeant bawled, grabbing at them. As they stood there, forlorn and deeply distressed, I noticed they were handcuffed in a strange way, with their arms chain-linked and then the hands secured. Our sergeant-major appeared.

'Yours, Sarge-Major, I believe?' said the MP. Without waiting for an answer he swung his arm around, finger pointing, to encompass the whole platoon, standing agog.

'Not one of you lot will speak to these bastards, nor attempt to give them any food – or you'll be in bloody trouble.' He glared hard at us as though waiting for his words to sink in. 'Your company commander is on his way to have a word with you. All yours Sarge-Major,' he said sharply, turning to the CSM and then climbing into his Jeep. As he pulled away he exchanged salutes with our company commander, who drove up in another Jeep. The major was grim-faced as he stormed over to Banger and Jock and then turned to us.

'I want you all to look at these two despicable creatures.' As he spoke he jabbed them with his cane. 'While we've been doing our duty, trying to keep Jerry off our doorstep, protecting our families and loved ones from the Nazi scum' – more prodding – 'these two snivelling wretches thought they would take a holiday' – prod, prod. 'Let me tell you all here and now, the Black Watch, a proud and honourable regiment, will not tolerate this behaviour. These two will be sorry. They'll make up for all they've missed, believe you me.' With a last disdainful look of contempt at the dejected prisoners he ordered the sergeant-major to carry on and was driven away.

There was some jeering and a few catcalls among the lads, and someone threw a couple of boiled potatoes at the deserters, but they were obviously past caring about verbal or culinary missiles. Being back among the HEs and Moaning Minnies was torture enough for them.

After a while I noticed our prisoners were missing, and when they reappeared a couple of hours later Shorty was detailed to guard them while they dug doovers. During a quiet chat with Banger he learned that the pair had been taken out on a patrol in no man's land with Jock's platoon and were manacled together the whole time.

At dusk my section was detailed to patrol and the prisoners

were ordered to accompany us – again handcuffed together.

'Make sure you return through this section,' our sergeant-major emphasized, 'otherwise you might get shot up.' As an afterthought he added: 'Mind you, if those two buggers play up, shoot 'em.' And he scowled at Banger and Jock.

As we set out the two prisoners were placed fifth and sixth in an eight-man section, making ten in all. Our mission was to listen for and observe enemy activity up ahead, prior to our attacking Le Havre in the morning. After creeping and shuffling for about a mile, stopping occasionally to listen, we lay down to rest. Although Banger and I had been good mates, I felt little sympathy for him in his present predicament, but I crept over to have a quiet word.

'How's it going, Banger?' I asked.

'What bloody good is this doing anybody, Whitey?' he asked tearfully. 'I'm past caring whether I'm killed or not.'

'Stick it out, Banger,' I merely said, and returned to my place behind the corporal. Banger failed to realize that his treatment was not only a punishment – harsh in the extreme, perhaps – but it acted as a powerful deterrent to anyone else in the company thinking of 'trotting'.

After an uneventful patrol we returned to our own lines. Saddled with our handcuffed prisoners, I shudder to think what would have happened had we run into an enemy patrol. We enjoyed a hot rum and cocoa, all, that is, except Banger and Jock, who were put in their doover, still handcuffed, and the entry hole covered. Thereafter our platoon spent a wretched night, due to noisy clanging tanks keeping us awake as they laagered in the farm area, ready for the Le Havre attack.

After stand-to at dawn our officer sent someone to attend the two prisoners. An NCO came rushing up, looking deadly white.

'Sir, sir, come and look – quick.' His anxious tone prompted several of us to follow the officer. He stopped with the corporal by the site of the prisoners' doover. Now it was a shallow crater littered with sods and pieces of shattered timber. Apparently as the tanks had pulled in during the night each one had swivelled hard on one track to take it away from our positions and into a suitable laager. Tragically each one had swivelled on the prisoners' doover, crushing Banger and Jock. For them the war was over.

Eventually, when time permitted, Banger and Jock would

have been court-martialled for desertion – after the company commander had shown us what happened to 'trotters'. But the plan had misfired badly.

As for me, once again I had to push these grisly events deep down into the innermost recesses of my mind; pack them in with all the other horrors. Switch off the light and forget them. If only it were that easy.

4 A Pleasant Interlude

At last the stalemate was broken. After building up reserves of men and equipment, in mid-August the Allied armies attacked on all fronts and the enemy was sent reeling. While the Americans on the right swept round towards Paris, gobbling up large areas of territory, the British and Canadians pushed north like a giant wave, sweeping the flotsam of a once-proud army before it. On and on the tidal bore rolled, liberating much of northern France and Belgium. But the enemy still held out in Le Havre and the 51st Highland Division was detailed to capture this valuable port.

We received the dreaded order 'Get dressed', signifying that soon we would be facing the enemy. Shorty, a little further up the line from me, shouted:

'Monty, you bastard! Give us a bloody break!' General Montgomery, the British Army Group Commander, though generally popular with the squaddies, was always blamed when we were ordered to attack.

Soon we were on our starter marks, with all sections and platoons in position, ready to move off. The tanks eased forward with the sections following just behind. We had barely started when we were halted and the senior NCO went among us.

'Come on you men, don't just lie around,' he barked. 'Check your mags, Bren gunners. The rest clean rifles and Stens. Make sure there's one up the spout, safety catch on till we move off.'

We squatted on the grass, the last tank of the armoured squadron just ahead of our point section. The hatch of the nearest tank flew open and two crewmen clambered out. Dropping down alongside the tank tracks they undid their 'flies' and proceeded to answer nature's urgent call. Corporal Grainger, lounging nearby, was wearing a huge grin.

'Put them things away,' he called out. 'Yer old ladies will go mad if they get shot off.' The two tankmen defiantly shook their 'wedding tackle' at him before 'adjusting their dress'.

'What's the hold-up then chaps?' asked the corporal.

'Dunno,' said one tankman. 'We're expecting something on the radio any minute.' Just then another crewman popped his head above the turret.

'Guess what?' he said excitedly, 'the squadron commander has refused to give the order to advance.' The two tankmen on the ground looked stupefied.

'Bloody hell! He'll be for it,' said one. The other came over to our lead section.

'And you know who he is, don't you?' he asked Corporal Grainger. The corporal shook his head.

'He's the brother of Lord Dunglass, who's in the government.' As the two men climbed aboard the Sherman one turned to us and shouted:

'Big brother won't be pleased, will he?' I later learned that the tank commander, Captain William Douglas-Home, brother of the future prime minister, refused to advance because he was appalled at the prospect of heavy civilian casualties in Le Havre. He was court martialled and sentenced to twelve months' imprisonment.

We all feigned diligence, tinkering with our various weapons to mollify the senior NCO. Private Al Smith was cleaning his Bren while chatting to his pal Corporal Tyas (Texas), who had become a father for the second time three days earlier. Since learning the happy news the corporal had not stopped talking about his new son. Our tanks began moving again and we received the order to get ready. Without warning a single shot rang out and Tex rolled on the grass groaning. Smithy stood paralysed, his face ashen. I was close by and dashed over to Tex, cradling his head on my knees. His normally ruddy face changed to a gun-metal grey with alarming speed and his eyes had a far-away look. In no time he was dead. It was almost as though he had been caught unawares by death. There was a bullet hole in his right side and intestines were dribbling out from a hole in the other side.

After cleaning the Bren Smithy had slammed the two halves of the weapon together and the loading mechanism had taken a round from the magazine and fired it, hitting Tex. Four of us carried our mate on a stretcher to a nearby barn, where we left him. Poor Smithy was in deep shock; he and Tex had long been close friends.

We moved forward again, with Smithy, eyes wide open with shock, joining our section. This was the second such incident involving our Bren gunner, who earlier in Normandy accidentally shot my close mate Ray Cheadle, a Northants lad. While the pair were sharing a 'slitter' one night Smithy became jumpy, convinced that someone was prowling in no man's land. To allay his anxiety Ray crawled out to investigate and finding nothing turned back. As his boots hit a metalled road just in front of our positions Smithy panicked and opened fire with the Bren. I was dozing in the next 'slitter' and heard the Bren fire and Ray's scream, but it all became entangled in a dream I was having. I heard Ray call my name several times as though from a great distance, and I began to shake, unable to separate nightmare from reality. Ray was rushed to the RAP, lucky to be alive. He had been holding his rifle at the port (across his chest) and two bullets had struck his hand, being deflected from his body by the rifle. A third bullet had sliced his shoulder. His hand was crippled, but he survived.

First Ray Cheadle badly injured, now Tex dead. As Smithy moved forward with us he seemed in a trance. In due course he was charged and reprimanded and later in the campaign was himself killed. I had a great deal of sympathy for him since the two tragedies must have preyed on his mind until the day he died.

After the blow of losing Tex under such tragic circumstances, our luck changed at Le Havre. First we entered the town without opposition, due to other troops from the division, and the 49th Division, doing all the hard work of winkling out the defenders. Then we learned that we would occupy houses hastily vacated by the Germans. There were bunks, showers, tables and chairs and, most important, a roof over our heads. This was indeed paradise, Shangri-La and Utopia all rolled into one after miserable weeks of hole-to-hole scrapping in Normandy through wind and rain, cold and heat, *Nebelwerfers* and 88s.

The mansion-sized dwelling allotted to our company stood in its own grounds below a huge rock massif into which large wooden doors had been set. But before exploring beyond the doors we had to remove, with great reluctance, our quarters' former 'residents'. These were local girls who had fraternized with the enemy and who were now seeking sanctuary from their own people, intent on retribution. As we escorted the girls on to a truck an angry crowd gathered, demanding we hand them over. There were some ugly scenes before we managed to throw a protective screen round the truck to keep the mob in check. But we were only delaying the inevitable as the girls were being driven to the local gendarmerie, where no doubt the town's elders would deal severely with them.

Sergeant Edmonds forced the enormous, iron-bound wooden doors in the rock face and we were staggered to find a labyrinth of tunnels running in all directions for hundreds of yards. In one huge section were twenty-foot-high racks holding countless boxes of stores, mostly tinned food, including tinned bread, which was indeed a rarity. Evidently Le Havre had been the main launching pad for Hitler's projected invasion of England and these stores were intended to supply his armies. The whole colossal set-up was a veritable Aladdin's cave, designed and built with typical Teutonic thoroughness. Behind more stout doors Old Edmonds found what he was looking for: the liquor store.

'Right, Whitehouse,' he said, turning to me. 'I'm leaving you on guard here. You'll be relieved in an hour.' He closed the door and looked hard at me.

'Nobody is to go near that door, got it? Tell 'em it's booby-trapped.'

'OK, Perce,' I said, 'but don't forget about me. I'm hungry and could do with a drink.'

'Wait a minute,' he said, and dashed back into the liquor store, returning a little later with a bottle. 'This is all I can find for now.' Then he disappeared again and brought back a tinned loaf and a large chunk of cheese.

'This'll keep you going for a while. I've got some business to attend to. Remember, tell no one what's in there, and the doors are boobied. OK?'

Highly excited, he ran off, leaving me with my 'reward'. I picked up the bottle and tried to read the label, but was baffled. Using my army knife corkscrew I withdrew the cork and cautiously sipped the liquor, which had a peculiar orangey flavour. I took a piece of cheese, had a bite of bread and then another swig. And so it went on. The tinned bread was rather dry and to compensate I drank more liquor. Sitting with my back to the door I munched and drank, feeling at peace with the world as all my cares drifted away. I must have passed out.

'Wake up, you drunken little bugger,' yelled Sergeant Edmonds, kicking my legs. I found it hard to focus properly, but managed to stagger to my feet, helped by four of my mates, who had accompanied the sergeant and who were now laughing at my helpless condition.

'Sit the stupid little bastard down,' said the sergeant. 'He's drunk half a bottle of Dutch curaçao.' While I lolled near the door the lads, from platoon HQ, and Old Edmonds entered the liquor store and reappeared carrying sacks.

'Now wait for me in the shadows by the tunnel entrance,' the sergeant told the lads, almost in a stage whisper. 'I'll just chuck this drunken bum on his bed.'

The next morning, feeling dry-mouthed but otherwise all right, I was put in the picture by the platoon HQ lads and learned what 'business' Old Edmonds had been transacting the previous evening. Our sergeant had organized a smuggling operation, selling rum from the store to local café and inn owners. These owners now wanted more of the spirits and so for the next three nights we did the 'smugglers' run', plying our furtive trade to shady and not-so-shady establishments. Each night the sergeant shared out the spoils and I was later able to send home a postal order for £25, a hefty sum considering that my army pay was only 21 shillings a week.

Following RAF raids on Le Havre, which had killed civilians and damaged property, we were ordered to avoid the town centre, for fear of the residents' hostility. But Bertie Bloomfield talked me into visiting the docks with him to watch American 'Seabees' repairing installations. We were surprised to find the locals quite friendly and, becoming bolder, we visited a café and then ventured into the town centre. One man pointed out a soil-filled plot on a footpath, which he said was the town mayor's grave. Apparently the mayor had been a collaborator and the Maquis had killed him without remorse, burying him beneath the pavement so that people could vent their anger by stamping on his grave as they walked past.

While chatting with this man we saw a Jeep carrying two MPs cruising along the main road past our side street. Then it reversed and the policemen eyed us suspiciously, dispelling any doubts we had about being out of bounds. All this time the Frenchman was talking volubly and gesticulating as only Frenchmen can. Without so much as an '*excusez moi*', we turned and bolted up the street. I glanced back and saw the Jeep in hot pursuit and the Frenchman standing agape, arms still waving madly. As we turned a corner, with the MPs following, I spotted a French woman about to close her front door after entering the house and in sheer desperation I shouted: 'In here, Bert.' I pushed the startled lady inside, we followed and I slammed the door. In my halting French I craved her forgiveness while trying to explain the situation. She understood and smiled sweetly. Through her net curtains we watched the Jeep halt outside the door and the two mystified policemen scratch their heads as they stared about them.

'Where the bleedin' 'ell have they got to?' we heard one say. It took great will-power for us to suppress our laughter and the lady of the house, who had entered into the spirit of the whole thing, was enjoying herself too. After cruising up and down the street several times and searching the vicinity the Jeep finally left.

The lady motioned us to sit and brought out a bottle of brandy and glasses and poured generous measures.

'*Victoire!*' she called, holding her glass high, and clinking glasses we toasted victory against the hated Nazis. For a brief but precious spell we forgot about the horrors of war, chatting amiably as the brandy coursed through our veins, producing a mellowing effect. It was heavenly sitting there in such a civilized manner, while all Europe – and indeed the world – was locked in a titanic struggle. My French stood up to the test, but Bert made no attempt to speak the language. He merely added an 'a' to the end of each English word, and strangely, the lady appeared to grasp his meaning.

Our hostess told us, with a tinge of sadness in her voice, that her husband had been taken away to work for the Germans three years earlier. At this news Bert's face lit up. He was a devil for the ladies – married or single, young or old – and the fact that the lady of the house had been without a man for so long did nothing to dampen his ardour. Soon he was holding the lady's hand, drawing her nearer to him, and they looked into each other's eyes with a deep longing.

'Aren't you due on guard at the hospital soon, Whitey?' he asked without taking his eyes off the lady. It was some time yet before my guard duty, but I got the message, and bidding our hostess *au revoir* I hastily left. Outside, I put my face close to the netted window and saw the lady leading Bert up the stairs, no doubt to paradise.

While standing guard outside the hospital I was badgered by local girls asking to visit their German boyfriends, lying wounded in one of the wards. But we had orders to let no one in and I had to turn them away. As my stint was coming to an end a small dapper man shuffled forward.

'How are you doin' Jock?' he asked, holding out his hand.

'Blimey,' I said, 'are you English?'

'Yeah, a Londoner. I've been here since the last war finished.'

'I bet you could tell a tale or two, old son,' I said.

The upshot was that he invited me to his house after my spell of guard duty, and Les Beach, who had accompanied my relief man, gladly accepted the invitation to join us. I never knew anyone as keen as Beachy to get his feet under the table. The house was quite small and similar to the two-up-two-down type in the industrial areas of England. Our host introduced us to his wife and four children, all looking much too young for him. Beachy and I were made most welcome and over tea and cakes our host related a horrendous story.

Earlier in the war scores of barges crammed with German troops left Le Havre to participate in landing exercises on the Norman coast (presumably they were rehearsing for the invasion of England). RAF planes, evidently tipped off by the Maquis or spies, flew over and dropped special bombs containing fuel oil, which covered the sea's surface around the barges. Other planes released incendiaries on to the fuel, creating a ring of fire, and then more bombs were dropped inside the ring. The little Londoner assured us that it was a massacre, with the soldiers' screams being heard by people miles away in Le Havre. He was a docker and learned that for weeks afterwards bodies were washed up all along the coast. Who knows? Perhaps this incident helped to convince the Germans of the futility of trying to invade England.

Two of our host's daughters offered to show us the cemetery where the Germans were buried, and after warmly thanking him and all his family for their hospitality we followed the girls.

Luckily they spoke good English and led us up a hill to the cemetery, which covered a large area. The wooden crosses marking the German graves were not placed at normal grave distance but packed shoulder to shoulder along the rows, each row only about three feet apart. One of the girls reckoned the cemetery contained more than 2,000 Germans – and many more must have been lost to the sea.

On our way back we took the girls to our quarters and loaded them up with tinned food and other goods from the 'invasion caves'. We promised to call again, but sadly we never did.

With much regret we now had to vacate our luxurious billets. They were claimed by the civil administration, who wanted to be near the enormous food supplies, which were to be distributed among the townsfolk.

'Our platoon is taking over a three-bedroomed house behind the hospital,' Sergeant Edmonds informed us.

'Wha', all thairty of us in one bleedin' hoose?' moaned Lance-Corporal Aitchinson, a Geordie.

'Well, you ungrateful bugger,' grunted old Percy. 'You can dig a bloody hole in the garden if you want, but I know where I'll be.'

Our new abode was elegantly furnished, with silk curtains and tasselled light-shades, and a delicious aroma pervaded the whole place.

'It sure smells nice in here,' I remarked casually while the lads were rummaging in upstairs bedroom cupboards and drawers, unearthing frilly panties and other exquisite underwear. One lad drooled over brightly coloured shoes.

'Oh God! Where are the girls?' he groaned.

'I bet they were the ones we shipped off in the lorries,' said Fred Cousins. I was still overcome by the powerful aroma.

'Cor! What a gorgeous smell,' I remarked again.

'Why the bloody hell d'you keep gannin' on aboot the smell?' asked 'Aitch'. 'Ain't y'nae bin in a brothel afore?' I was momentarily speechless, but quickly recovered.

'Yeah, of course I have,' I lied. 'But it wasn't as nice as this.' I was at great pains to hide the fact from some of these characters that I was still a virgin soldier. They would have gone to extreme lengths to initiate me.

Among all this frippery Mushty found his cushion. It was a beautiful thing, made of patterned silk, edged with lace and filled with the softest down, and it smelt divine. To him it was a tangible link with the life we had all pushed out of our minds. In the coming months he would be found most nights during his two-hour stand-down fast asleep on the bottom of his muddy hole with his head nestling on his magic pillow. Despite threats and orders from NCOs to discard it he clung on to the pillow and would have killed anyone who tried to take it from him. I am not sure how far Mushty carried his beloved cushion, stuffed under his leather jerkin, but two sections of our platoon were ambushed after the Rhine crossing at the village of Speldrop, and most were killed. I heard that Mushty was among the dead, and if so I feel sure he would have clutched that pink perfumed talisman to the end.

I went downstairs and into the garden of our new billet to find Mushty holding a plump hen by the legs.

'How about us getting this bird cooked for scoff tonight?' Mushty asked his good mate, Fred Cousins.

'It's a big bugger,' said Fred. 'Where are we going to get it cooked? And who's going to pluck and draw it? Not me mate.' Mushty was crestfallen.

'How about over the road at the hospital?' I suggested, hoping to get in on the deal.

'Why yeah,' said Mushty, eyes now gleaming. 'They must have the facilities. Will you take it over, Whitey?'

'No, but I'll come with you,' I said. I had no desire to venture alone into the underground hospital and risk getting waylaid by the German orderlies. But first the bird had to be killed.

'Hold its wings above its back with one hand, Mushty, and grab its legs with the other,' ordered Fred, who came of good country stock. He looked round the garden and found a hefty stick.

'Right, Mushty, hold her tight. Here goes,' said Fred, wielding the stick. Thwack! He brought it down sharply on the bird's head.

'Fuckin' 'ell, Fred,' said Mushty, hastily dropping the bird on the ground, 'it's crapped all over me.' As the stick connected the bird ejected a white stream over Mushty's neck, chest and arms. Those of us watching – and a number had gathered by this time – were convulsed with laughter.

Fred calmly picked up the quivering bird, slit its throat with his army knife and hung it on a nail in the fence.

'Give it half an hour to drain, then take it over to the Jerry cook,' said Fred, still laughing.

Later, after Mushty had spruced himself up a little, he and I went over to the hospital, where the German orderlies eyed us with a mixture of hate, contempt and curiosity. I smiled at one wearing a white coat and beckoned him over.

'You cook this for us, please?' I asked, pointing to the bird Mushty was holding. 'What you want – cigarettes, chocolate to cook this?' He hesitated for what seemed an age, then an amused smile played about his mouth.

'OK, I do it for you,' he finally said. 'What time you want?' It was about two in the afternoon.

'Five o'clock,' said Mushty, holding up his open hand.

'OK, see you five hour,' said the orderly, taking the bird. As we walked back Mushty was rubbing his hands in eager expectation.

'Ho, ho, chicken tonight,' he said, skipping along, 'and we've got a nice bottle of wine.'

But we should have known better. What would we squaddies have done if the roles had been reversed? We would have played football with the bird, urinated and stamped on it, and then thrown it in the oven with its feathers on – which is pretty well what the Germans did with our hen. When we went to retrieve the bird every orderly we questioned merely shook his head and continued working. Then one simple-minded German eventually opened the oven door.

'Ah, dis,' he said, pulling out the tray. Mushty was livid. On the tray was what looked like a piece of scorched lorry tyre, glued down.

'What the bloody hell's this?' yelled Mushty, grabbing the tray.

'*Nicht gut*, eh?' said the simpleton.

'*Nicht* fuckin' *gut*,' screeched Mushty, barely able to control himself. He flung the tray at the German, who scurried behind some racks. We looked around; all the Germans had vanished. I could see the funny side of it, but Mushty was about to explode and it took all my powers of persuasion to coax him away before he wrecked the place.

'German bastards,' he kept muttering as we made our way back.

The whole platoon had a good chuckle when we related the

details of our adventure. Percy Edmonds expressed surprise at our naivety.

'You didn't really think they'd cook your bleedin' dinner, did you – after them nursing hundreds of their mates we've helped put in the hospital?' He shook his wise old head in disbelief.

'I tell you what,' he concluded, 'if they'd thought a bit harder they could have cooked you a lovely bird, golden brown – and then laced it with poison. There's bound to be some in a hospital. I reckon you've been bloody lucky.'

'Weren't we prats?' said Fred seriously. One to you Jerry, I thought, but you missed a good chance.

After seven or eight restful days we somehow managed to tear ourselves away from Le Havre. The war trumpets sounded and we had to return to the ghastly business of fighting.

The floodgates were now wide open and the inexorable tidal wave of armies rolled on through France and into Belgium and Holland, washing over the Wehrmacht's elite divisions as they limped and staggered back to the fatherland. Such was the general euphoria among the lads that rumours circulated of a total victory by Christmas. But while the British Second Army and the Canadian First Army continued their drive north, our battalion, as part of 154 Brigade, was sent to Dunkirk, where a strong enemy garrison stubbornly held out.

September's 'season of mists' and vivid autumnal colours had succeeded high summer by the time we made the long journey in lorries across France, a distance of 200 miles. We passed through areas reminiscent of England, with cows grazing contentedly in rich, rolling pastureland, and farmers tilling the soil after the harvest. These landscapes, untouched by war, spoke eloquently of serenity and permanence and made me yearn for the old country and my family.

Our role at Dunkirk was merely to lay siege to the town and tie down its garrison. The Germans had ringed the whole area with a deep collar of mines and miles of barbed wire, effectively sealing themselves in. It was a 'stand-off' situation, although they shelled us and we retaliated. After our gunners had sent over one heavy barrage they received a message from the enemy that shells had landed near the hospital and could we please be more careful.

The Maquis were active in the area and with their knowledge

of the countryside proved helpful. They were installed in farmhouses with enormous, ancient-looking machine-guns, and in fact several stayed in the farmhouse allotted to our platoon. One was a glamorous young lady who acted as a courier, flitting about the country lanes on her cycle, constantly ogled by sex-starved squaddies.

With our artillery fire increasing, a twenty-four-hour truce was arranged to allow the evacuation of several thousand civilians from the besieged town. Some of us went with our officer to the barrier and watched the people streaming out, pushing handcarts, wheelbarrows and prams laden with precious belongings. German soldiers stood on the other side of the barrier to witness the exodus and exchanged words with our officer. We learned from them that our company sniper, Brummy Robinson, who had vanished a day or two earlier, was now a prisoner. We were able to pass his mail and some 'goodies' over to his captors for delivery. It all seemed very civil and courteous, though there was no question of fraternization with the enemy.

The Maquis interrogated many of the refugees, punching and beating some and locking others in a barn. We thought it brutal, but were told not to interfere in these internal squabbles. Three hours before the official truce was due to expire the barriers were replaced and the Germans withdrew. Soon afterwards a message came from our forward OP that the Germans were digging in several fields beyond their original positions. Back came the answer from battalion HQ: 'If they can break the truce, so can we. Move up a couple of fields.'

The wheels were quickly set in motion and within an hour we were up front lying in ditches alongside a road, accompanied by the minesweeping personnel of our S (Specialist) Platoon, who would sweep a six-foot-wide lane and mark it with white tape. But the mines had been sown thickly, and in the dark, with a strong breeze coming in from the sea, it was exacting, time-consuming work locating each device, scraping round it, checking for boobies, and then gingerly lifting it out.

Time was running out; soon it would be midnight, when the truce expired. Our officer therefore ordered us to start digging in in the cleared section, keeping strictly within the taped corridor.

Sergeant Edmonds was with us and not in the best of moods.

Earlier he had been drinking with other NCOs in a nearby inn, hoping to sleep off the effects of the strong local liquor before the truce expired. Now he had been dragged out on this farcical, face-saving escapade, none too steady on his feet. Only the darkness saved him from being severely reprimanded by our officer. We who idolized him found his antics hilarious as he staggered about in the dark, falling over other squaddies and cursing.

Three 'slitters' had been dug and the 'sweepers', followed by our officer, then Old Edmonds, and finally Beachy and me, slowly edged forward along the tape. Suddenly there was a loud click and someone yelled 'Down!' Beachy and I flung ourselves into one of the finished 'slitters', landing heavily on the crouching occupants.

'What the –' Their startled cries were drowned by a vicious explosion, followed by screams and shouts. With everyone's movements restricted by the nearness of mines a certain amount of panic ensued. We were not aware of it at the time, but the strong wind had blown the white guiding tapes off alignment, resulting in our walking on ground not cleared. Someone had trodden on an 'S' mine, one of the enemy's more diabolical devices. Foot pressure activated a spring, shooting the body of the mine (about the size of a large tin of beans) into the air. The mine exploded at face height, discharging a hail of ball-bearings with devastating effect. After his drinking bout Sergeant Edmonds was too slow to take evasive action and caught the full blast. He died by the roadside ditch on that black, windy night. His face was destroyed and his throat torn apart by the ball-bearings. Mercifully it was too dark to see the full scale of the horror as we dragged him back along the 'safety corridor'.

The plan to steal a couple of fields during the truce was called off and we crept back to our farmhouse positions thoroughly dejected, feeling like felons caught in the act. It had turned out to be a stupid, needless fiasco with two S Platoon NCOs and their officer badly wounded and Sergeant Percy Edmonds dead. Old Edmonds had been killed within sight of those same Dunkirk beaches from which he had been rescued four years earlier. I prayed that he had gone to join his 16-year-old son, who after all was just as much a victim of Dunkirk. And I spared a thought for his wife, somewhere in Buckinghamshire, who would no doubt suffer untold agonies on receiving that fateful telegram from the War Office.

Percy Edmonds had been like a father to me, guiding, chastising when necessary, advising and comforting. He would be sorely missed. Farewell Percy. RIP.

5 A Woodland Foray

After our inglorious efforts at Dunkirk – inglorious so far as our platoon was concerned – in early October we were relieved by the Royal Tanks and Czech troops and set off to join the rest of the division, by now established in Holland. Dunkirk would remain besieged until the end of the war, our top brass no doubt assuming that it was not worth the expenditure of precious soldiers' lives.

Following the British Second Army's rapid advance through France and Belgium and into Holland, culminating in the valiant but costly and unsuccessful Arnhem operation, we paused to catch our breath and lick our wounds. In any case the Germans, fighting now on their own doorstep, had bolstered their defence and were proving a tougher nut than ever to crack.

One cold, damp night soon after arriving in Holland, with the battalion in the line, our platoon was stretched out in fields parallel to a metalled road about twenty yards to the rear. We had an excellent view of no man's land, which was lit by 'Monty's Moonlight'. Our boffins had hit on the ingenious idea of bouncing searchlight beams off low-lying clouds to illuminate the enemy's positions and no man's land. This artificial moonlight worked well during these autumn nights, with thick cloud cover acting as an ideal reflector. On this particular night German flares were also active, keeping us fully alert.

I heard unusually noisy footsteps on the metalled road just behind us and looking round saw, with the aid of the simulated moonlight, Black Watch bonnets and hackles and German helmets intermingled. The Jocks were quite vociferous, though not loud enough for me to distinguish the words. I assumed our boys were escorting prisoners to the 'pen'.

'Where are you taking that lot?' I called out. This was the

signal for pandemonium to erupt. Firing began, with bullets zipping past us, followed by shouts and screams. Three Germans rushed off the road into the field between our section's 'slitters', obviously unaware of our presence, and we opened fire on them. Silhouetted against 'Monty's Moonlight', they were easy targets and soon fell. I could see and hear a scuffle in the road, with much grunting. Apparently several of our lads had jumped a German officer and between them managed to kill him with their bare hands.

Later I heard the full story. It seemed that an enemy patrol penetrated to our company HQ and captured about six of our lads. The Germans tipped what they thought were two jerrycans of petrol over our Bren carriers and stores and lit a match. Luckily for us they had mistaken water for petrol. (The two cans were almost identical, but the petrol containers carried a red disc.) The noisy walking I had heard on the road was caused by our boys scuffling along holding up their trousers after the Germans had removed their bootlaces, belts and braces. Nevertheless, it did not prevent them turning the tables on their captors when the opportunity arose. My sudden call to the group must have panicked the Germans.

The Dutch countryside hereabouts, bisected by numerous canals and streams, was flat, desolate and almost featureless, with just an odd isolated farmstead dotted here and there. During a bout of enemy shelling while we were up front in this remote region, a panicky cow fell into a 'slitter' and broke a leg. When the shelling had stopped two of our lads caught the distressed animal and tied it to a tree. Having recently become our platoon's Piat man, I carried a .38 revolver and was now asked to end the poor animal's misery. The Enfield .38 revolver Mark 1 was the standard army side-arm from 1936, but its inaccuracy was legendary. As one wit put it, you could barely hit the sea from a dinghy. But I thought there would be no problems with a cow. As I took aim at the animal's forehead someone cautioned:

'Mind the bullet doesn't ricochet back, Whitey.' I stepped back another pace or two and someone else said:

'Oh, I'd give it a bit more room.' I moved back just a little more and from seven or eight feet took careful aim at the centre of the cow's head and fired. The shot penetrated the eye, but seemed to have little effect. I fired again and the bullet went into its nose. A third shot hit it just above the eye and the cow remained standing. I was upset at inflicting even more pain on the tormented animal and pleaded with someone else to kill it. Up stepped a Pole who had somehow attached himself to our unit. He snatched the .38 from me, pressed it to the animal's forehead and fired. The animal immediately slumped down – out of its agony. Even before it hit the ground the Pole drew his knife and slit its throat. He reached in for the jugular, severed it and the blood gushed out. To speed the process he jumped up and down on the cow's side. It was an excellent piece of butchery, and in fact we later learned that he was a butcher by trade. Gradually he acquired bits of our uniform and was eventually accepted by our cooks. We ate well on beef for several days after the killing.

We were on the move again and, passing through Eindhoven, followed a good metalled road that led to the small town of Schindel. On the outskirts of the town we drew rein before two farmsteads, one each side of the road. The farms were recced and to our surprise were pronounced clear. By now it was dark and our platoon hastily dug in around the right-hand farm while 5 Platoon took the farmstead on the left.

After a quiet night we stood-to at dawn, the enemy's favourite time for attacking. There was a golden rule about stand-to while up front: nobody left his 'slitter' until the stand-down order had been passed by word of mouth along the line. Anyone at ground level during this time was deemed to be the enemy and liable to be shot at.

Following stand-down we washed and shaved, ate and slept, but with one man from each 'slitter' always fully alert – usually in two-hour stretches. Later in the day we were cheered by the sight of our cheeky little Lysander spotter plane chugging backwards and forwards over the front. We could be sure that he would warn us of any signs of an imminent German attack. The frail aircraft, though flying low and slow-moving, was never fired on – probably because the enemy knew the pilot would radio back the positions of any gun flashes to our artillery. He finally waggled his wings and flew off towards our rear.

An hour or so later Lieutenant Yates and an artillery officer, the FOO (Forward Observation Officer), with his field phone, entered the farmhouse in deep conversation, and on emerging several minutes later informed us that our spotter plane had reported the enemy positions too close for comfort.

'We're going to stonk them out with our artillery,' they told us. 'Stay in your "slitters" during the shelling. It's rather close, but with their low trajectory our 25-pounders should do it.'

The two officers returned to the farmhouse, where they were spotting through a hole they had made in the roof by removing tiles. I was sharing a 'slitter' with my mate Beachy and we crouched low waiting for the fun to start. Soon half a dozen shells came over to land a good hundred yards to our front. There was a pause while the FOO, in touch by phone with the gun end, readjusted the range. Then the commotion started. When a shell lands nearby there is no whistling or screaming, just a sudden sharp rush of air before the bang. And so it was now. Simultaneously with the loud explosions the earth – fortunately between our 'slitters' – erupted in a series of fountains, showering us with dirt, stones and sods. The farmhouse roof received a hit, sending tiles in all directions, and our two officers came hurtling out of the door, covered in dust and debris. They dived into our 'slitter', which was handy, and Beachy and I had to squeeze up tightly to allow them in. Our lads cowering below ground were furious.

'What the fuck's going on, you dozy pricks?' 'You silly pair of bastards,' 'Bugger off, you ten-mile friggin' sniper,' were some of the more polite comments that reached the officers' ears.

'I think we'll try and shift the Jerries some other way, if you don't mind,' Lieutenant Yates told the FOO.

'OK old chap, suit yourself,' he replied before leaving us.

'Sorry about that, you two,' said our officer, apologizing to Beachy and me. 'I'd better go and calm the other lads.' And he scrambled out of our trench to soothe some extremely frayed nerves.

Corporal Burke, whose section was furthest forward and had suffered some very near misses, crawled back to us. He was livid.

'I'm sure there's no fackers out there. The plane must have spotted Jerry's old positions. The fackin' idiots!' We had seen nothing of the enemy all day, despite his supposed nearness. Perhaps Burkey was right.

I was dug in on our platoon's extreme left and could see 5

Platoon's positions just across the road, about thirty yards away. Occasionally we gave each other a reassuring wave.

At dusk a truck pulled in to the farm area and dumped coils of barbed wire, which we were told to unravel across our front and round the perimeter edges.

'Seal yourselves in for a while, explanations later,' was the message from our NCOs. Our other platoon across the road was also laying out barbed wire and we were puzzled, since this was all new to us. Nevertheless, when we were sealed in, with tin cans hanging from the wire to warn of prowlers, we felt infinitely more secure.

Word went round that the evening meal was being served up in a barn in 5 Platoon's area and I crept back for the usual stew and tea. I stood in line behind an old friend, Danny White, who had joined the 1st Bucks Battalion in Scotland about the same time as me. On D-Day he was a lance-corporal, but now he sported the pips of a first lieutenant, having won his commission in the field. Danny was a likeable young man, worshipped by 5 Platoon. It was typical of him to queue with the other ranks, instead of sending a batman to fetch his rations.

We chatted about our platoon's shelling earlier and while I tried, with a show of bravado, to laugh it off, he expressed concern and was pleased to hear that no one was hurt.

'What about this barbed wire?' I asked. 'Looks like the 14–18 war all over again.'

'So you've not been told yet?' I shook my head.

'Perhaps after your meal someone will fill you in. We've just come from an O Group. It seems Jerry is well dug in close to us, and it may be a good idea to come at him from behind. So the Argylls are pushing on tonight, then looping left to take him from the rear, and he'll be caught in the middle. If he makes a break through our lines the barbed wire will check him. Not a bad idea, hey?'

Sure enough, after we had eaten and settled in our 'slitters' our NCOs explained the plan Lieutenant White had earlier outlined. At about midnight heavy firing broke out on our right, and the sky turned red while we watched and waited, thankful that we were not involved. All through the night the noise of battle had us keyed up and as stand-to time approached the whole platoon was already fully alert.

'Thank Christ Jerry's gone the other way,' said Beachy,

echoing my own thoughts. No sooner had he spoken than a burst
of automatic fire came from 5 Platoon's area just across the way.
This was followed by shouts and screams, figures flitting about in
the early morning mist and more firing. Unsure of the situation in
this poor light we held our fire. There were anxious shouts from
'slitter' to 'slitter' in our platoon as the lads enquired what was
happening. From our position, nearest 5 Platoon, Beachy and I
were able to reassure everyone that we were in no immediate
danger.

But now the Germans were through 5 Platoon's barbed wire,
firing into the 'slitters' and sometimes falling alongside them. My
.38 revolver was useless even at this range of thirty-odd yards, but
Beachy took pot-shots with his rifle at the nebulous figures
moving through 5 Platoon's patch.

The firing had died down when a lone figure ran between the
trenches, firing. Immediately half a dozen guns blazed away at
him and he faltered, staggered and fell. All went quiet. Suddenly
there was movement to our front. It was the Argylls, advancing
cautiously in the tricky light. Corporal Burke jumped up with joy.

'Ho! Ho!' he laughed. 'It's the Argylls.' Then I heard an Argyll
shout 'Enemy front' – the standard call – and crack! – a single
shot rang out. Burkey tumbled back into his 'slitter'.

'Hold it! Hold it! Black Watch here,' we yelled. Corporal
Burke's 'slitter'-mate groaned loudly and in a distressed voice
cried out:

'Burkey's copped it – right in the forehead.' It had been a wild,
unlucky shot in the murky light. Members of the section ran over
and lifted the corporal out, but he was beyond help. Another
tragic incident would be kept from the folks back home.

The Argylls came among us, looking haggard and weary after a
hellish night. We knew the stress and tension they must be
suffering, having undertaken similar night forays ourselves. Two
German prisoners, loaded with the Jocks' Piat bombs and Bren
pouches, were shoved and prodded in no uncertain manner. The
corporal in the point section was Jackie Evans, from Smethwick,
an ex-Bucks man I knew.

'Blimey, Jacko,' I said to him, nodding towards the prisoners,
'they're earning their corn.'

'Yeah,' he said, forcing a grin, but still showing signs of the
night's ordeal, 'better them than us. Anyway, it'll make 'em think
twice about doing a runner.'

The details of 5 Platoon's firefight came to light when I visited them later. As the Argylls attacked, about twenty Germans were squeezed towards the platoon's positions. Eight had been killed – three on the wire and the other five as they dashed between the 'slitters'. Unfortunately five of 5 Platoon's lads – those in the forward trenches – had also been killed. The saddest news of all was that Lieutenant Danny White was among the dead. It was Danny I had seen stagger and fall as the skirmish was ending. In his eagerness to get at the enemy he had committed the cardinal sin of leaving his trench during stand-to and in the poor visibility his own men had cut him down.

Sadly Corporal Burke likewise broke the golden rule of not staying low during stand-to. He was a popular lad and a fine soldier, best remembered perhaps for being caught with his pants down – literally – by a Russian back in Normandy.

Before moving off later that day we went to view the positions from which the Argylls had ousted the Germans. They were certainly close to our lines – about forty yards away – and well dug in under a dry ditch. Had we attacked from the front we would not have seen them and they could have slaughtered us after we had passed. So, although we lost some good lads that night, the Argylls' action had probably saved many more lives.

Our company was halted about a mile short of a bridge while our officers held an O Group. The outcome was that our platoon had orders to send a six-man recce patrol to assess the enemy's strength in the bridge area. Back in France our depleted company had been reinforced by men of the Tyneside Scottish, a Territorial battalion of the Black Watch, and eight of them (six Geordies and two Welshmen) were assigned to our platoon. The Tyneside Scottish had landed soon after D-Day, as part of the 49th West Riding Division, and because of their affinity with the Black Watch were already wearing the red hackle in their bonnets.

The eight who joined us were friendly, but bitter and angry towards the hierarchy, maintaining that they had been used needlessly as cannon fodder in Normandy. In the past malcontented battalions and companies had been broken up with the men scattered among other units, and I wondered whether this had happened to the Tyneside Scottish lads. On the other hand their losses could have been so severe that disbandment was the only option. Our new men related lurid tales of fierce encounters with the SS and Panzers at Villers Bocage, in Normandy, where casualties on both sides had been heavy. Their hatred of the enemy was more pronounced, more bitter than anything I had known.

These eight remained intact as a section in our platoon and were chosen to recce the bridge, but only five were available; one more was needed.

'Wee Whitey'll gan along, he'll no' mind, will ye Whitey?' said Sergeant Baxter. In the past I had volunteered for patrols and was now paying the price. Earlier it had been a big thrill, but now I was wiser and more fearful of what might happen. Nevertheless, I felt I had a reputation to maintain and reluctantly nodded agreement to Sergeant Baxter's suggestion, though my stomach had tightened and I could feel my heart pounding wildly. My only consolation was that the five Tyneside lads accompanying me certainly knew how to look after themselves.

Corporal Grainger, the leader, had such a strong urge to get to grips with the Germans that he would glare across no man's land at them, his eyes filled with an intense hatred. He never wore a steel helmet – his own peculiar way of showing utter contempt for the enemy. Lance-Corporal Aitchinson had a lilting Geordie accent, so broad that sometimes I could hardly understand him. He walked with a gangling, comical gait, but was fearless and extremely wise. There were two other Geordies in the patrol and Private Edwards, a Welshman, completed the number.

We moved off in single file, the corporal and two Geordies leading, followed by Lance-Corporal Aitchinson, then me, with Taffy bringing up the rear. Soon we entered rather dense woodland and after cautiously advancing for five or ten minutes the corporal motioned us to gather round him.

'I'm not keen on this single file idea,' he whispered. 'We'll split into two threes and keep going through each other nice and steady. At least three or four pairs of eyes will be looking round while the others leap-frog through.' This seemed a better idea and Aitch, Taffy and I pushed through to the front. After stalking forward warily for several minutes, eyes and ears atuned to the slightest deviation from normal, we signalled the other trio to overtake us. In this way we made good progress through the woods, but the tension was beginning to tell on me. My heart was thumping again and I could feel the sweat oozing out all over my body, running down my face and into my eyes, until it impaired my vision. The respite in Le Havre had been most beneficial, soothing my tattered nerves, but now all the old symptoms were returning with a vengeance. The slightest crack of a broken twig underfoot, or the sudden passage of a bird through the trees turned my legs to jelly. I sensed that fear was getting the upper hand again, and was becoming a more determined and pugnacious adversary than the enemy.

We paused for a breather and to check the map, wondering how much further we should probe before returning. Taffy suddenly cocked his head and looked back the way we had come. Grainger and Aitch, heads together, were muttering over the map when Taffy put one hand over the sheet to attract their attention and pointed to the rear. We peered anxiously through the greenery and my heart must have skipped a beat. Ambling towards us, following our trail, were a dozen or so Germans, about thirty yards away. By their nonchalant, carefree attitude, with weapons slung over their shoulders, it was obvious they had not seen us and were not expecting trouble. Our corporal, calm and complete master of the situation, gripped his Sten and leaned over to Aitch.

'You come with me,' he whispered, 'and the rest of you stay here. And for God's sake don't fire unless you hear me start shooting. Then get anything that comes your way.'

The two NCOs melted away to the left and were soon lost among the trees, leaving the four of us waiting and wondering. My throat was so dry I could hardly swallow. We looked at each other with misgivings as the enemy approached ... fifteen yards, now ten. I was waiting for Grainger and Aitch to come behind them and yell '*Hände hoch*', the signal for the rest of us to step out and show the enemy that they were surrounded and that surrender was their only option. But it was not to be. Violent bursts of Sten fire came from our left, destroying the deathly hush that was always an integral feature of no man's land. The Germans half turned in panic, trying to unsling their rifles, but the unrelenting fire chopped them down. Above the firing we could hear cries of pain that were abruptly cut short, ending in gasps and groans. Now the rest of us fired into the group, sending the field-grey figures milling around and stumbling.

Within seconds it was all over. We stood there motionless for what seemed an age, but was probably less than half a minute.

I crept forward as Grainger and Aitch emerged from the trees and caught my breath as a German slowly raised himself from the long grass, hands held aloft. We were within a couple of feet of each other and I marvelled at his extreme youth. His pale, frightened face seemed so fresh, without a blemish, and his eyes pleaded for mercy. By one of those strange quirks of fate our helmets were camouflaged with American parachute silk of the same pattern. Two more shaken but unhurt Germans stood up with difficulty and raised their hands. While Taffy and I stood over them, they tended another of their number, lying seriously wounded. In the meantime the two Geordies mooched about, prodding the motionless figures sprawled in the long grass. Corporal Grainger called me over.

'Pick up that Schmeisser, Whitey. It'll be just the job now you're Piat man.' I eased the bloodstained automatic weapon from a German officer's grip and took four magazines from his satchel. Aitch relieved the officer of an important-looking attaché case slung around his neck.

'Right, let's get back,' said the corporal. 'I've nae much bloody ammo left.'

'Me neither,' chipped in Aitch. I looked at the bodies, some spreadeagled in grotesque positions.

'Eight,' I counted to the NCOs.

'Yeah, they owe us much more than that, the bastards, but it'll do for now,' said Corporal Grainger. Aitch merely nodded. I glanced at the NCOs' faces, which somehow seemed different, as though the blood-letting had eased the tension, relieving their pent-up feelings. They looked at each other and exchanged tight little smiles. Perhaps sweet revenge had brought about this remarkable change, which made me wonder just what had happened at Villers Bocage.

Our three prisoners carried their wounded comrade back to our own lines, where Corporal Grainger related events to Lieutenant Yates. As he spoke we heard a loud explosion from the direction we had come; the Germans had blown the bridge.

Later that day I quietly asked Lance-Corporal Aitchinson why we did not take the Germans prisoner instead of opening fire.

'Ach, Whitey,' he answered in his lilting, scarcely

understandable Geordie dialect, 'we didna really know how many were aboot, did we? There might have been mair of the buggers behind 'em. Yer better to shoot the bastards while ye can. They would, och aye mon. Ah know they would have shot us – ay've seen 'em.' So that was it really. Take no chances in this game, said the voice of experience.

I jealously guarded my Schmeisser, cleaning it regularly and learning how to strip it down. It would later save my life.

6   The Crossroads Skirmish

We were 'somewhere in Holland', as the folks back home were told, somewhere in this flat, dismal countryside, but as usual we infantrymen were completely ignorant of our whereabouts. We saw an occasional signpost that gave us only a rough idea of where we were going, or where we had been. After the heady days of late August and September, when our victorious armies had swept all before them, progress in late October was painfully slow. Enemy resistance had stiffened appreciably as we neared the Third Reich's borders, and to compound our problems the weather had turned cold and wet with frequent mists hugging the landscape.

We had slogged all day across fields and through woods, not seeing much of the enemy, but feeling his presence as shells and mortar bombs frequently sent us diving for cover. As darkness fell – it seemed to get late very early, as one wag would say – we approached a village that was ablaze. Here we paused just outside the fireglow range, not wishing to make targets of ourselves. The company runner hurried to us, calling quietly for Lieutenant Bernard, our officer, and the lieutenant then asked section leaders to report.

'Orders are,' he said to the NCOs in a low voice, '4 Platoon move to the left, 5 Platoon to the right. We're 6 Platoon, going straight on. Beyond the fires is a crossroads – that's our objective. Seven Section is point section and leads off. The Piat man goes with you. That's it. Any questions?' There were no questions, so 7 Section lit out, with me as Piat man trailing behind, alongside Private Pope ('Popeye'), my bomb carrier and protector.

Seven Section comprised Corporal Holland (Dutchy), Lance-Corporal Fitzsimmons and Private Ken Ware (the Bren team), and Privates Ken Holden, Blondie Marsh and two new lads who had joined us only that day and whose names I did not know.

Our platoon's Piat men had moaned so much about the weight of the weapon that I had volunteered to take it for a spell. The Piat (Projectile Infantry Anti-Tank) was a four-foot bazooka-type infantry weapon that fired a 2½ lb bomb and had proved effective against Panzers at up to one hundred or so yards. Its main problem was in re-cocking. A powerful spring launched the bomb, but to reset the weapon the spring required a squaddie with the strength of Hercules. To attempt reloading in action was extremely difficult, though the firer's oppo (the bomb carrier) was there to look out for him. The Piat man's official weapon was a .38 revolver, but I now had the German officer's Schmeisser, which I had lovingly nursed since acquiring it. The Schmeisser (MP40) was a beautiful all-metal sub-machine-gun – probably one of the best of its kind ever made. It had a 16-round magazine (of which I had four), and its folding stock was unique at that time.

Lieutenant Bernard joined 7 Section, walking alongside Corporal Holland as we slowly advanced. Our latest platoon commander had replaced Lieutenant Yates, recently promoted and transferred to another company. He was rather small, with a pencil moustache (they seemed to be the stock-in-trade of wartime subalterns), and I had the impression he was not a true infantry officer because he often asked our opinion on matters appertaining to the infantry that he should have known. But for all that he was a gentleman through and through and we respected him.

As we became silhouetted against the firelight I was fearful of snipers and my old apprehension returned a hundredfold. But the dreaded moment passed as we eased forward, with the darkness now our friend. Lieutenant Bernard signalled us to get down and then disappeared with the Bren team, leaving the rest of the section crouched on the damp grass, eyes strained into the pitch-black night. He was soon back, in a cheerful mood.

'Another thirty yards chaps, cross the lateral road up ahead, and Corporal Holland will show you where to dig in. It seems quiet, but take no chances.'

'Right sir,' we whispered, moving forward in a sort of creeping crouch. We were now well and truly in no man's land, which called for ultra caution. Sure enough Dutchy awaited us as we crossed the lateral road.

'OK lads,' he whispered, 'I'm about thirty yards up the road with Fitz and Ken on the Bren. Whitey, you and Pope dig in around here, on this right side of the road, two of you site your 'slitter' ten yards up on the opposite side, and the other two another ten yards up on the same side. Got it?'

No problem, I thought, as we set about digging our trench. On each side of the road was a thick hedge under which ran a three-foot-wide ditch, half full of water. Running parallel to the ditch was a grass verge, and it was here, a couple of feet in from the ditch, that we started digging. But after going down about three feet (the regulation was four feet) water began seeping in from the ditch. Cursing under our breath at these sodden conditions we decided to make the trench wider to compensate for the lack of depth. In this way we could at least crouch down or kneel. Popeye and I settled into our soggy 'slitter' comforted by the thought that we were some thirty yards behind the front men with the Bren. It is a daunting, often terrifying experience looking out across no man's land, knowing that there is nothing between you and the enemy.

Sergeant Baxter appeared around midnight.

'Grub up,' he whispered. 'Just one of you fetch both lots.' Then after a pause: 'Everything OK?'

'Nothing but flamin' water round here,' said Popeye. 'We can't get our "slitter" deep enough.'

'Yeah,' I chipped in, 'we're practically swimming in it.' The sergeant, always cool and fearless, merely gave a quiet chuckle and moved on to check the others. Sergeant Baxter and I had become quite friendly since his taking over from Old Edmonds, the drawback being that he insisted I accompany him on patrols or the laying of trip-flares in front of our positions.

Popeye went back to the QM truck for our food. When the quartermaster and his boys drove up with our rations they were always a 'blur of activity' and I had to laugh at the indecent haste with which they dished out the food before scurrying back to the relative safety of the base as though the whole German army was hot on their tail. Popeye returned with our stew and tea, moaning as usual.

'How do they expect anyone to live on this bloody stuff? Nothing but rubbish. My pigs get better grub than this.' Popeye, from Kent, thought he had managed to avoid the army by working on his brother's farm. But the Land Army girls usurped him, and now he loathed all women – especially those in the Land Army. He was hardly soldier material, especially the infantry. Unmarried, portly and with thinning hair, he would have found his vocation in a shoe shop or a tailor's.

We sat on the edge of our 'slitter' dangling our legs just above the muddy bottom and made short work of our lukewarm stew and cold tea. Afterwards, back in the trench, Popeye put his head on his chest and blew out his cheeks.

'Get some shut-eye if you want, Popeye,' I said.

'D'you think we're all right?' he asked, looking down the road into the inky blackness.

'Yeah,' I said, trying to sound convincing. 'Fitz won't let anything slip by.' Lance-Corporal Fitzsimmons, of Bristol, a member of the Bren team stationed a little further up on our side of the road, was a reliable lad whom I liked. Corporal Holland was different. In his mid-thirties and frail looking, he had a wife and three children, and come what may he intended returning to them when it was all over. He was one of the few men I knew who carried a clean white handkerchief and he often said:

'I shall do my duty, but if it comes to "do or die", I'll wave my hankie.' I thought that reasonable enough. I could understand his attitude. It was a pity that married men with families had to face the sharp end.

While Popeye settled back I prepared for a long vigil. I stared hard down the road into the night, but it was so dark I could not see our nearest neighbours, Blondie and Holden, only a few yards further up on the opposite verge, though I could hear their muttering. Earlier I had placed my small pack and .38 revolver in its belt at the front of our 'slitter', with the prized Schmeisser on top. To the left was the Piat, loaded and cocked, and on the other side were the three spare Schmeisser magazines and a grenade. A deathly hush descended on the landscape. There is no place more eerily quiet than the front line and no man's land at night, unless perhaps it is the graveyard, although even there birdlife and other nocturnal denizens begin to stir when the rest of the world sleeps. Here, not even a mouse would venture from its hole, as though it sensed that dark deeds were afoot this fateful night.

Stan Whitehouse while with the 1st Buckinghamshire Battalion

(*Top*) Landing craft aground on the Normandy beaches. (*Centre*) British infantry cross the Caen Canal Bridge after its capture by men of the 6th Airborne Division. (*Right*) British troops watch a farm building blaze after entering a French village

(*Top*) Men of the 51st Highland Division disembark on Sword Beach. (*Centre*) British infantry in a sunken lane fire on enemy positions. (*Left*) British troops cautiously approach an enemy-held village

(*Top*) Squaddies taking cover in trees before an attack. (*Centre*) British infantry in snow-covered positions in the Ardennes await the order to attack. (*Right*) Men of the 51st Highland Division stalking through the Reichswald Forest.

A squaddie of the 1st Black Watch digs in on German soil

The German town of Goch after bitter house-to-house fighting

A squaddie takes a
well-earned catnap in
his 'slitter'

A boat patrols in the flooded 'island' region of Holland

Stan Whitehouse sporting the Black Watch tam
o'shanter

A rare moment out of the line. Left to right: Les Beach, Stan
Whitehouse, Les Shorthouse relaxing in the Monty Club, Brussels

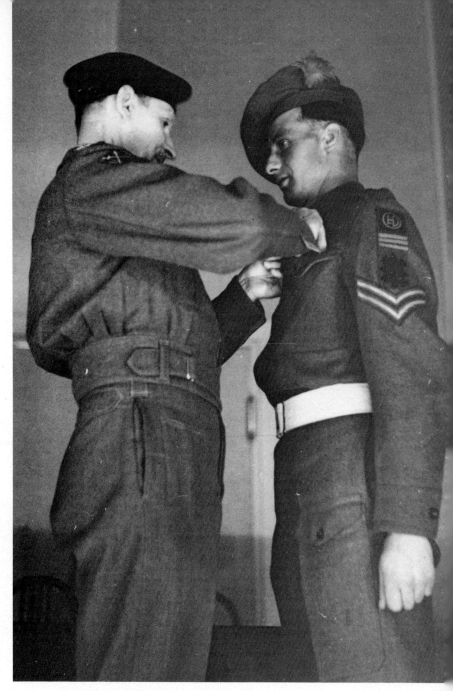

Corporal Les Shorthouse (Shorty) receiving the Military Medal from
Field Marshal Montgomery

Popeye began snoring gently and his steady breathing seemed to relax me. Ah well, come the dawn and the Argylls or maybe the Gordons will pass through us and we will have a day or two to gather our wits, write a couple of letters and get some sleep. 'Shut-eye' was still the squaddies' number one priority. I began nodding off and to keep awake I stood up in the trench, but the glutinous mud came over the tops of my boots, sticking me to the spot. With some difficulty I freed myself and clambered out. From the ditchside I pulled long tufts of grass and threw them into the trench, though I longed for a couple of duckboards, like they had in the earlier war's trenches, to keep my feet dry.

While treading down the grass I thought I heard a metallic 'clunk'. Standing up in the trench I paused. There it was again, faint, but unmistakable. I peered into the night, eyes strained to the utmost. My heart gave a flutter as I saw a German helmet, then another and a third against a sliver of silver skyline. Each one appeared for a brief moment and then vanished. (It transpired that the Germans were walking along the ditch on the other side of the road and as they crossed a small earthen bridge – allowing animals access to the fields – their heads rose above the hedgerow, giving me a glimpse of their helmets against the lighter skyline.)

Where was the Bren team, who should have been dug in almost opposite the Germans? Why were they not firing? (I was to learn later that the Bren's firing pin was broken, which explained the metallic clicking I had heard.)

'Enemy front!' I bawled. 'Enemy front!' Pointing the Piat towards the silhouettes I fired. A mighty explosion erupted down the lane, followed by weird shouts and screams. Training now took over. After firing at night move your position or hide. Being unable to move I ducked. It was not a second too soon. A long burst of the dreaded Spandau raked the front of our 'slitter', hurtling my small pack, pouches and pistol over my head and away into the night. Luckily the Schmeisser, its spare magazines and the grenade fell into the trench. The enemy were now roaring, as though making a charge, but were still invisible. I stuffed the spare magazines into my blouse, grabbed the Schmeisser and emptied it in their direction, spraying it from side to side. Even before the firing stopped there were more screams and guttural shouts. I looked down at Popeye, who all this time had been crouched low in our 'slitter'.

'Why aren't the other buggers shooting?' I gasped. He just stared grimly into the gloom. I heard more German voices, as though orders were being shouted. Changing the magazine, I fired again and was surprised at the amount of flash and sparks coming from the automatic. Realizing that these would pinpoint my position I emptied the magazine and ducked.

Swoosh! I felt the wind on the back of my neck as a Panzerfaust (a bazooka) bomb skimmed the top of our trench and exploded in the hedge.

'Jesus Christ! Popeye,' I gasped as we crouched low, 'that was bloody quick – and spot on.' A guardian angel must have been watching over me that night. Had the Spandau not whipped my pack away earlier the bazooka bomb would have exploded on hitting it, and that would have been the end of us.

I stood up quickly, finished off the magazine and crouched again. There was barely time to draw breath before another bazooka bomb zoomed in, showering us with dirt. I was now too terrified to be frightened – if that makes sense. I felt I was about to be killed and there was nothing I could do about it. To combat my 'bomb-happiness' I stood up and hosed another magazine down the road, this time finding relief by shouting, 'Come on you bastards, come on.' I was becoming hysterical, but the shouting seemed to release a pressure valve and I clipped on another magazine – the last – and emptied it in the general direction of the enemy.

'Come on you Hitler bastards, come on,' I yelled as I fired. The adrenalin was surging through me in waves and I was thrilled that we had checked the attack. Popeye now stood alongside me, though still not firing. All this time he had been slumped in our 'slitter' and I thought he was dead. But I was still worried about our lack of support.

'Why aren't you shooting, 6 and 8?' I called out to the other sections. There was no answer.

'For fuck's sake help us out,' I pleaded. Utter silence. Had they been overrun? I wondered. I turned to Popeye and was about to comment on our mates' failure to help us when I heard a roar and turning quickly saw a huge German rising from the opposite ditch and pointing a Panzerfaust at us. I froze as he climbed out and crossed the road towards us, snarling and uttering horrible guttural sounds. I was convinced that this was my last moment on earth. In sheer, futile desperation I picked up the grenade and threw it at him without bothering to pull the pin; in any case, he was too close. The grenade hit his body and bounced away.

Screaming deliriously now he was on the edge of our 'slitter', still pointing the bazooka at our heads. Like two puppets on the same string Popeye and I simultaneously jerked our hands in the air and croaked '*Kamerad!*' But the German made a fatal mistake by ignoring our offer to surrender. Had he ordered us out of the trench we would have complied readily. Instead he emitted a ferocious bellow and lifting the bazooka high slammed it down on our heads. As the weapon connected with my steel helmet I felt a tremendous jarring through my whole body, my knees buckled and every atom of breath was forced out of my lungs. I recall groaning, 'Oh Mum' – and then blacked out. Old sweats say that at such moments a man's life flashes before his eyes. Mine did not, but photos of my mum and dad and brothers and sisters, in my battle-blouse pocket, became imprinted on my mind. I must have been out for seconds only and came round kneeling in the trench and pushing hard to ease the helmet off my sore, throbbing head. But for the helmet such a blow would surely have smashed my skull. Popeye was again lying slumped in the trench.

I could hear desperate, panicky cries coming from nearby, and as objects gradually registered I saw two figures thrashing frantically in the water-filled ditch alongside our 'slitter'. The big German was now trying to hold one of our lads under the water, though I could not see who it was. Some unknown force compelled me to climb out of the trench, in slow motion, it seemed, grab my Schmeisser, and close in on the German. Bent low, with his powerful hands holding one of my mates down, he was unaware of my presence. The sub-machine-gun was empty and I therefore had no killing weapon, the thought of which drained my confidence. Nevertheless, I raised the Schmeisser and smashed it down with all my strength on the German's helmet. It was useless; the blow glanced off the helmet and struck my mate. The German never flinched. I tried again, with the same result. Christ, I thought, I'm killing one of my mates. A head appeared above the water, gurgling and spluttering.

'You're hitting me,' a thin voice cried out.

The next blow had to count. This time I reversed the gun and, holding it by the barrel, aimed for the German's curved spine, the only part of his body that seemed to be exposed. The Schmeisser's pistol grip had a steel band edging and it was this that I brought down with all the force I could muster on to the big brute's backbone. He screamed with pain and straightened up, clutching his back. I was vaguely aware of his victim, still coughing, crawling away into the gloom.

Standing upright, this Goliath of a man turned on me. His face was blacked up, accentuating the whiteness of his teeth, which he gnashed in pain and anger. His eyes too were white, startlingly white and evil-looking as he glared at me. He stretched out his massive arms towards me and I tried to step back. But my feet stuck in the mud, and now, bereft of all strength, I fell back with a splash into the ditch. He leaned over me as I cowered under the hedge and then I heard a distinct 'pop', which seemed no louder than a cork exiting a bottle. With a grunt the German staggered, and grabbing at his side keeled over alongside me. I looked up and saw Popeye holding his smoking rifle. It was the first shot he had fired all night. But what a telling shot! Without it I would not have survived. Now my tormentor lay beside me, moaning with pain. I scrambled out of the ditch and dashed back to our trench, where I showered Popeye with thanks.

'I'm supposed to protect you, ain't I?' he said dryly in his Kentish brogue. Ken Ware was sitting on the bank nearby, groaning and holding his head while blood ran through his fingers. Then I realized it was Ken the German had been trying to throttle – or drown – in the ditch. I was distraught at the state of my mate.

'Ken, oh Ken,' I cried, moving towards him.

'You were hitting me, Whitey,' he sobbed. He could have blasphemed me in his anger, but that was not in Ken's nature. He was a lovely, gentle bloke who never swore, and who seemed wholly out of place in this tough combat business. It must have been mental torture for him. I helped him to his feet, apologizing profusely.

We had not yet finished with Goliath, as Popeye and I christened the giant German, who was fumbling with his clothing under the water. He was so big that even when sitting on the bottom of the ditch the water barely covered his waist.

'Watch him, Popeye,' I said. 'He might have a pistol.' My oppo deliberately levelled his rifle at Goliath, who stopped fumbling and began talking incoherently, though I recognized the words 'doctor' and '*kaputt*'. But we had too many problems of our own to tend to his needs.

'Get to the medics,' I said, turning to Ken, 'and find some bugger in our platoon HQ. Tell 'em we need help. We've no ammo, there's only me and Popeye, and we haven't a bloody clue what to do next. By the way,' I continued after a pause, 'Where's Dutchy and Fitz?'

'They were hiding in the hedge,' he groaned. 'The firing pin broke on the Bren.' I was about to say: 'But they had Stens', then decided against it. I pushed Ken towards the rear.

'Sorry again mate, but at least it'll get you a few days out of this,' I consoled him before he staggered away. I could hear him calling softly, 'Don't shoot, don't shoot,' as the night engulfed him. Good bloke, I thought. After all that shooting some trigger-happy squaddie might open fire rashly at the sight of an obscure figure lurching towards him.

I spotted my equipment, half in, half out of the water. My water bottle had taken a burst of Spandau fire and looked more like a colander, but my .38 revolver was intact, and meagre fire-power though it was, it boosted my deflated confidence. I climbed back into the 'slitter' alongside Popeye and thanked him once more, nodding towards the German, who had begun moaning and fumbling again with his clothes. Perhaps he was trying to stem the bleeding.

'That bugger makes me nervous messing about like that,' said Popeye.

'Hey, Fritz,' I snarled angrily at him, aiming my .38 at where he was fiddling. 'You – pistol here.'

'*Nein. Nicht Pistole*, Tommy,' he groaned. '*Doktor*, Tommy, *Doktor.*'

'You should be so lucky,' I muttered.

It was still dark. How long the little battle had lasted it was impossible to say – five, ten, fifteen minutes. I had no idea. I could make out several obscure bundles lying in the road, quite still save one that appeared to move occasionally. I heard a clanking noise in the distance that sounded ominously like a tank – a Panzer maybe, I thought, shuddering. Then I heard a voice from the rear:

'It's Sergeant Baxter, Whitey.' Our sergeant was grinning broadly as he approached, but on seeing him so cheerful my anger and frustration boiled over. Rightly or wrongly I thought it diabolical that Popeye and I had been left to battle it out alone, with no one even bothering to contact us. I saw nothing to grin at and something inside me snapped.

'Why didn't we get any fucking help?' I exploded. 'Six Section is there, 8 Section there,' I pointed out, 'and not a fucking shot fired to help us.' I was seething now. 'We've no fucking ammo, there's a Jerry on the road up there rolling about and this bastard in the ditch might have a pistol.' I gave vent to my rage in no uncertain terms.

'We've just heard a fucking tank moving about and God knows where the rest of our section is,' I concluded.

Sergeant Baxter, old Desert Rat that he was, let me get it all off my chest.

'Calm down, Whitey, calm down,' he said softly. 'Nobody fired because they couldn't see what was happening through the hedges. They might have shot you if they had. You and the Jerries were all mixed together,' he added, glancing around. 'As for these buggers moving around, we'll shoot 'em.' So saying he fired two short Sten bursts at the prone restless figure I had indicated up the lane. Then he turned to Goliath, who was now trying to pull himself up using the hedge. I noticed the Russian Front ribbon on his chest, which we had come to recognize on prisoners filing back.

'No, no, don't shoot him, Sarge,' I said, knocking the Sten off its aim. Baxter just grinned.

'He'd have no bloody mercy on you two,' and he brought the Sten up again.

'No, Sarge,' I pleaded. 'He's no danger now. Don't shoot him.'

'*Nein, nicht schiessen! Ich kaputt,*' said the swaying German.

'Righto, it's up to you,' said Sergeant Baxter, lowering his Sten. 'You two have done very well. The boss will be pleased. And I'll take this bugger away for you.' He moved to the ditch, knocked off Goliath's helmet and dragged him by the hair on to the road.

'I'll send Shorty up with another Bren – and a drop of rum. OK?' Then he left us, dragging the groaning prisoner mercilessly behind him.

'My word, you're a big chappie, aren't you?' I heard the sergeant say as they departed. Goliath's cries of pain continued to reach us long after they had gone.

I had a sneaking admiration for my adversary. He was tough

and he had tried to kill me – the bastard – but inexplicably I wished him well. For some days afterwards I turned over in my mind whether to report his bravery to my superiors, but like many a good intention it came to nothing.

As Popeye and I settled back into our muddy 'slitter' an aura of tranquillity settled over the area, affecting me deeply. After letting off steam to the sergeant and getting rid of the fidgeting Goliath I was much calmer, feeling lucky to be alive, but at the same time completely drained, devoid of all energy. My head still throbbed from Goliath's mighty blow and I felt a physical and mental wash-out.

The mystery of my mates' disappearance continued to puzzle me. I refrained from calling out lest I give our position away and in my fatigued state – more mental than physical – I was not brave enough to crawl out and investigate. I assumed the rest of 7 Section must be dead or prisoners. My main worry was our lack of fire-power. The Schmeisser was useless without ammunition and the Piat was hardly suitable for close-quarter combat. We were left with my .38 revolver and its six rounds and Popeye's rifle. I thought about leaving Popeye out here and going back for help, but decided it would be unfair to ask him to remain on his own. We mulled these possibilities over and in truth decided that if attacked again: 'He who ups and runs away, lives to fight another day.' Then we heard a scuffling of feet on the road just ahead.

'Oh for Christ's sake, Whitey, the bastards are coming again,' yelled Popeye. We could take no more and scrambled out of the trench, tensed up and ready to run for it.

'Don't shoot, Tommy, please don't shoot,' said a voice in impeccable English.

'What the bloody hell's that?' whispered Popeye as we strained our eyes at a white object approaching. As it drew near we saw it was a large white sheet held between two Germans. A third man walked in front but to one side, shining a torch on the sheet. I lifted the .38 and Popeye levelled his rifle.

'May we talk?' said the man holding the torch. He wore the standard German white vest bearing a large red cross. We were taken aback by this unexpected turn of events.

'What d'you want?' I asked, my voice trembling.

'Can we send our wounded soldiers over to you?' he answered, again in perfect English. I could have kissed him.

'Of course you can,' I said eagerly, trying to emulate his rendering of our language. He turned and signalled with his torch to the two men holding the sheet and they dropped it, revealing the wounded, lined up in pairs. It was as though a conjuror had shouted 'Hey Presto' to complete his *pièce de résistance*. The wounded, with bandaged arms, legs and heads, looked a pathetic lot and were obviously still in shock. I was surprised at their number – sixteen in all; my Schmeisser must have caught them full on as they charged.

I always thought the German helmet – derisively called the 'coal-scuttle' – with its heavily curved rim in front of the ears, the most sinister looking of all helmets. Remove his helmet and the mighty Wehrmacht warrior looks far less terrifying. With this in mind I made a point of 'de-helmeting' any surrendering Germans I saw. And now, while Popeye covered me with his rifle, I went along the double row of prisoners throwing their helmets into the ditch. It gave me great satisfaction to see their frightened, pained faces, these ruthless men who had conquered almost the whole of Europe. As I walked among the prisoners I was struck by the distinctive smell of new leather and wondered whether they were raw recruits.

I had just completed the job when out of the darkness came my great pal Shorty, who had brought us a Bren and half a bottle of rum.

'You're making enough bloody noise up here, Whitey,' he joked. 'What the hell's going on?' He pushed his helmet back and laughed.

'They're sending their wounded over,' I answered. 'D'you want to take them back?'

'Yeah, sure,' said Shorty. 'Come,' and he beckoned to the front pair, who stumbled after him, followed by the rest.

'Tell the major it's a present from 7 Section,' I called after him.

'Right,' he answered before vanishing with his herd of prisoners.

My message 'from 7 Section' was really a distortion of the facts. No one from 7 Section was around. As the Piat man I belonged to platoon HQ and went wherever I was sent. But I could not foresee the consequences of my 'misrepresentation of the truth'.

As dawn began to break a mist descended, making the whole

scene even more ghostly than during the night. I heard footsteps that heralded Lieutenant Keeble, from company HQ. With hands in his greatcoat pockets, collar turned up and a Sten tucked under his arm, he looked as though he was out for a stroll. He stopped at our 'slitter'.

'Come along, Whitehouse. The Jerry Red Cross chappie reckons the rest of their mob will pack in if we ask them.'

'Well why doesn't he go and fetch 'em?' I asked.

'He's afraid some fanatic – or maybe the SS – will shoot him if he returns,' the lieutenant said. I was unhappy about this whole business and offered more excuses.

'The same fanatics might shoot us,' I reasoned.

'Oh stop making bloody excuses,' snapped Lieutenant Keeble, losing his patience. 'Get out and follow me. I'm telling you everything will be OK. Now out! Come on!' I reluctantly left the 'slitter' and using the lieutenant's body as a shield, walked directly behind him. He chuckled at my action, but adopted a more serious attitude as we reached the German corpses lying in the road – seven in all. These were the soldiers killed when I fired the Piat. The lieutenant peered closely at each body, trying to determine how the men had died.

'You've had a lively night, Whitehouse. I think there'll be a medal in it. There's no blood or marks on some of these,' he added looking rather puzzled as he prodded each one with the muzzle of his Sten. I had noticed a bicycle, twisted somewhat, lying on the ditch bank.

'I think my Piat shot must have hit the bike, sir,' I said. 'The blast would have seen them off.' It seemed that three had in fact been killed by the blast and the others by shrapnel.

Just a little further on we saw the bodies of the two Black Watch lads who had joined us the previous day. The lieutenant and I studied them more closely.

'Poor buggers. Looks as though they were knifed or bayoneted,' he said. I felt myself going cold all over.

'Bloody hell sir, I can't even remember their names,' I said. The officer shook his head in despair as we moved on.

'Where are those bastard Jerries?' he snapped, obviously as upset as me at the sight of our two dead mates.

I was still mystified by the absence of Dutchy and Fitz of the Bren team, and Blondie Marsh and Holden, whose 'slitter' had been sited on the opposite side of the road from ours, a little further up. As there was no sign of their bodies I assumed that they were now prisoners.

Lieutenant Keeble and I turned a bend in the road and there were the Germans, looking demoralized and no doubt ashamed, but relieved, I should imagine, to see us. The lieutenant never took his hands out of his pockets.

'Come along you chaps, come come,' he called out cheerfully, and slowly, glumly, the wretched men ambled towards us. I rested my hand on the .38 but did not draw it. This is stupid, I thought. Although the Germans had already discarded their weapons, we would have no chance if one had a concealed pistol and started shooting. I forced a smile and decided to try the 'de-helmeting' routine.

'*Bitte*,' I said smiling, pointing to one young German's helmet. He looked nonplussed and I tried again.

'*Bitte*,' and this time I motioned to him to remove his helmet. Still puzzled, he handed it to me and I flung it down. Eventually they all realized what I wanted and complied. Again I was struck by the overpowering smell of new leather, though in this case any new recruits were mixed with more seasoned campaigners because several were wearing the Russian Front ribbon.

Lining them up in pairs, we headed back down the road towards our lines. Good old Popeye had tea brewing on his Tommy-cooker when we reached our 'slitter'.

'All right if I stay here, sir?' I asked.

'Yes, OK,' answered Lieutenant Keeble, 'and just remember the date, Whitehouse, in case anything comes of this.'

'Righto sir,' I said, and as he turned to escort the prisoners back I called out:

'By the way sir, I haven't a clue. What is the date?'

'Er ... let me see ... umm ...' The lieutenant thought deeply. 'Oh yes, it was the 27th yesterday.' I stood transfixed. 27 October.

'Hey, Popeye,' I called out. 'I was eighteen yesterday. Put a drop of rum in that brew.' My oppo handed me a mess tin of tea.

'Drink yer tea. You'll be bloody lucky to see nineteen.'

About mid-morning recce patrols reported that the Germans had pulled back and when another company moved through us we could relax a little. I was most surprised to see Dutchy and Fitz, who told me that when they discovered the Bren was useless they broke through the hedge into the field beyond.

They had thought it best not to move for fear of getting shot by either side. Blondie and Holden, who also joined us, had likewise escaped through the hedge, but on the opposite side, when the Germans attacked. In the circumstances I suppose it was the wisest move. I tried to forget that they all had Stens and plenty of ammunition. At least I felt that I had proved myself, which meant a great deal to me.

The depleted section lay on the grass recounting the night's turbulent events, all jabbering away like crazed men – the delayed result of our brush with death. Dutchy suddenly stopped talking and began shaking from head to toe, biting hard on his lip to stop ... what? Screaming? Cursing? It seemed to be the signal for reaction to surface generally as the rest of us trembled unashamedly. Wide-eyed we looked round at each other, unable to control our emotions. We knew it had to emerge; it was fear. The fear endured during those night hours, the fear of what lay ahead.

Corporal Dutchy Holland was awarded the Military Medal for 7 Section's defence of the crossroads, during which seven Germans were killed and thirty captured. Lieutenant Keeble, Sergeant Baxter and Shorty all protested strongly to the CO, claiming that the award should have gone to me. But it was too late; the citation had already been submitted. Dissatisfaction among the lads over the award reached the ears of our company commander, who sent for me.

'The message we received with the prisoners was that they were a present from 7 Section,' he explained apologetically. 'It was a section award and as Corporal Holland was NCO in charge of the section he got the gong.' Ah well, that's life, I thought, but I would have liked that MM, especially for my dad.

Poor Ken Ware had seventeen stitches in his forehead after my clumsy efforts to save him from the clutches of Goliath. He returned to us about a month later, still complaining of dizziness when he bent down. Sadly Ken met his death rather ignobly – from our own gunfire – later in the campaign as we assaulted the Siegfried Line.

Three years after that fierce little battle of the crossroads, when, during my life and death struggle with Goliath I had cried 'Oh Mum', my family and I were celebrating my twenty-first birthday. We were discussing the war years and where we were on particular birthdays when my mum revealed a most singular occurrence. On the night of my eighteenth birthday she had a vivid and frightening dream in which she saw me scrabbling in the mud. Then she heard me cry 'Oh Mum' and sat up in bed, covered in sweat. She was unable to eat or sleep for days – until she had received a letter from me, indicating that I was safe. I was stunned by this revelation, all the more so because I had told no one at home about my frantic skirmish that night. Undoubtedly psychic powers were at work on my eighteenth birthday, collaborating closely with my guardian angel.

7 Old Pals Meet

Before the war the village of Helmond, near Venlo, with its
double row of neat cottages and small gardens, must have been
quaint and attractive. Now, as we rumbled in aboard Kangaroos
(Sherman tanks converted into troop-carrying vehicles) the
village looked a sorry sight, its buildings damaged and
pock-marked by shelling, and the gardens badly neglected.
German long-range artillery greeted us and hastily vacating our
vehicles we sheltered behind the wall surrounding a cottage.

'Jerry must have left,' gasped Beachy between bursts,
'otherwise they wouldn't be shelling the place, would they?'

'You never know with these buggers, do you?' said Shorty.
'Come on,' he added, 'we're off.' Our officer, Lieutenant
Bernard, had detailed 6 Platoon to take the row of cottages on
our right while another platoon concentrated on the opposite
side. The only firing as we closed in was from the long-range
artillery, which had us hitting the ground as shells whistled over
our heads. But the cottages were empty, with not even a sign of
the locals.

Our next objective, a larger stone-built house fifty yards or so
further on, had a wire fence which the enemy had strengthened
with coils of barbed wire.

'Watch this place,' called the lieutenant. 'It looks like their
HQ.'

'Touch nothing – it could be boobied,' joined in Sergeant
Baxter. 'Spread out,' he added. 'Take your men round the back,
Corporal Holland.' We scampered after Dutchy, terrified of
Spandaus in our exposed position.

'Right, you lot – through the wire,' ordered Dutchy.

'Anyone got any cutters?' asked Beachy.

'Yeah, I have, but they're in me pack, and I'm not bloody

hangin' round here cuttin' that stuff,' said Dutchy. So we carefully picked our way through the barbed wire. While I was straddling the fence, precariously poised, a big buxom lady appeared at the back door of the house and waved to us.

'Hey Tommy, here,' she called out. In my eagerness to join the other lads I ripped the seat of my trousers while trying to negotiate the last strands of wire, and could feel an uncomfortable draught as I approached the back door. The lady had broad shoulders and massive, sinewy arms, and judging by her ruddy complexion she came from country stock. My first impression was that I would hate to tangle with her in a dark alley. But she had a pleasant smile and welcomed us most warmly.

'Are you Dutch?' I asked her.

'*Nay, nicht Deutsch – Hollander*,' she answered, somewhat offended, scowling at me. I was initially perplexed, but then realized that these people refer to themselves as '*Hollanders*'. 'Dutch' was similar to '*Deutsch*', their name for the Germans. No wonder she looked hurt by my question. She, and all the people in this area, had an intense hatred of the Germans, who had totally wrecked their lives since overrunning the country nearly four-and-a-half years earlier. The locals referred to the enemy contemptuously as the '*Mofferman*', which roughly translated meant a tramp or a hobo.

Once inside the house we realized why we had seen no villagers: they had all taken shelter in the cellars of this more substantial building, and now emerged to greet us with vigorous handshaking and hugging before returning to their own homes.

The buxom lady, who presumably lived in this large house, saw me examining the tear in my trousers and brought out an enormous needle and what looked like baling twine. She beckoned me to remove my trousers, which prompted loud guffaws and ribald remarks from my mates. But I was adamant: the trousers stayed on, whereupon the lady, after much chiding and admonishing with a wagging forefinger, grabbed me and I was forced on to a large table, face down. Soon the big needle was deftly weaving in and out, watched by the whole inquisitive, expectant section.

'Don't move, Whitey, or your goolies will be stitched to your shirt,' one wag warned.

'I reckon she's SS, with orders to sew your cheeks together,' someone else remarked. And so the lewd comments were tossed back and forth as the buxom lady, while prattling away and with an elbow dug sharply into the small of my back, repaired my trousers.

Suddenly Sergeant Baxter clicked his heels and came to attention.

'Room 'shun!' he bellowed. Still prostrate on the table, I swivelled my head as far round as possible and saw my mates spring to attention. I tried to follow suit, but the elbow dug deeper into my back.

'Still, Tommy, still,' the buxom one censured me. Out of the corner of my eye I saw an officer resplendent in brown leather and red trimmings. He was a brigadier, no less, looking as though he had just stepped out of a Savile Row window. Despite the staff officer's presence the brawny seamstress stitched merrily on. The brigadier looked at Sergeant Baxter and then at me.

'What's this, running repairs?'

'Yessir, sorry sir, she won't let me get up,' I said weakly.

'Yes, I'd do as she says if I were you,' he answered, smiling at my friendly helper.

It seems we were right in assuming the house had been used as a German HQ. Now the brigade staff wanted to sift through important looking documents left behind by the retreating enemy. We moved to an even bigger establishment, complete with riding stables, owned by a haughty couple who would not even condescend to look upon lowly squaddies. Despite the war, with its manpower shortage, they continued to employ a large staff of menials, and they also owned two dalmatian dogs they said were called Monty and Ike, in defiance of the Germans. However, the locals soon unmasked these renegades. During the German occupation the couple were regarded highly in Nazi circles and successfully pleaded for their buildings not to be used as a military headquarters in case they were bombed or shelled. And as for the dogs, their true names were Adolf and Hermann. Soon after our arrival the couple were taken away by our military police and charged with being German agents.

Our platoon was advancing across the Dutch countryside when the lead section requested smoke from our mortar man before tackling a suspicious looking stretch, where an ambush was feared. My mate Beachy was the two-inch mortar man at the time, but had been drinking looted wine a little earlier which rendered him rather tetchy. He crept forward to the edge of the stretch in question, where our officer awaited him.

'Put some bombs over there, Beach,' he ordered.

'No sir, I'd put them over there,' interjected Sergeant Baxter, pointing in a different direction. The officer and the sergeant, in trying to assess the situation, taking into account the wind direction and other factors, had a divergence of opinion. Their 'over here', 'over there' discussion continued for several minutes and I could see Beachy becoming more and more exasperated, his face growing redder and redder. Finally he exploded.

'Who's in charge of this fucking mortar? Me or you two? I'll put the fucking bombs where I think they ought to go.'

Our officer was dumbstruck, unsure how to handle matters, but Sergeant Baxter, an old hand, defused the situation with a little tact. All of us lying nearby cheered when we heard my mate letting off steam and it helped ease the mounting tension. Beachy eventually put the smoke bombs where he thought they should go and the smokescreen worked well.

The battalion reached the outskirts of Waspik village in Kangaroos. Eight of us were crammed into the converted Sherman tank with just the driver and machine-gunner up front. As we rumbled through the streets anxious faces appeared at the windows – an understandable but risky reaction from the locals. We were all keyed up and trigger-happy and a strange face peering at us was liable to receive a Sten burst.

We slowed to a crawl and the lead Kangaroo opened fire with its Besa machine-gun. An explosion followed almost immediately and we were showered with dust and smoke.

'What the hell's goin' on?' Beachy, sitting next to me, called to the Kangaroo in front. To add to the confusion two Germans with raised hands stood up in a ditch alongside our vehicle. They were festooned with leaves and twigs – a beautiful camouflage, but rather incongruous among the rubble of Waspik. No one knew what to do about the prisoners; we were afraid to leave the Kangaroo in case some not-so-friendly Germans appeared.

A wounded German lay between two houses about twenty

yards away and I pointed my gun at him. He waved his hands as if to say 'Don't shoot.' Evidently our lead tank gunner, firing at enemy troops mining the road, had exploded a mine, causing a large crater up ahead that impeded our progress.

'Everybody out,' came the shout from up front. Our section jumped out alongside the two surrendering Germans, who lay down with us in the roadside ditch. Someone took the prisoners away for questioning and Beachy and I crept forward in search of the wounded German spotted earlier. He had vanished, so we inched round to the large crater in the road. Private Eddie Head and his mate were looting gory German bodies, caught by the mine blast and scattered around the crater. We were sickened to see Eddie hacking at the fingers of one corpse with his army knife to remove the gold rings.

'Eddie, you bastard, I don't believe this,' I said, feeling revulsion at his callousness.

'There's some bloody good rings here,' said Eddie, quite unabashed. 'Some other bugger will have 'em if I don't.' His mate gave a chuckle as he pocketed a watch and various trinkets from another body.

'You must be bloody hard up to lower yourself to that,' said Beachy, equally annoyed.

'You pair piss off,' retorted Eddie, now quite riled. 'If these bastards had managed to get the mines planted we would have copped it, not you two, and the bastards would have looted us, so fuck off, both of you.' We left them desecrating the bodies and returned to the ditch to await orders.

Several streets and gardens still had to be cleared and a Sherman tank waddled forward to support us. Sergeant Baxter organized us into an arrowhead formation with the tank leading, our section tucked in behind, and another section on each side, just a little behind. Amazingly civilians tagged along, obviously not aware of the danger to themselves. The Sherman managed to skirt the crater and we made steady progress until halted by another explosion just ahead. We were stunned and deafened momentarily, but otherwise unharmed. The dust and smoke still lingered when Shorty, immediately behind the tank's right hand track, leaned out and fired three rapid shots. A foolhardy German, armed with a Schmeisser, had rushed forward, intent on disposing of us before we had recovered our composure, and my mate's shots had blasted him on to his back, only feet from the Sherman.

Fully alert now, our section dashed for a house on the left, unsure whether it was an enemy strongpoint. Once inside we combed it, teeth clenched, swearing hysterically and dripping sweat. At rare moments like this fear became submerged, and with a rush of blood I was buoyed up as though on drugs, finding boldness in the support of the rest of our section. Two of our lads who had bravely ventured upstairs called to us urgently and on joining them we looked out of the window and saw what had happened. Up ahead, on a bend in the road, was a low-growing shrub behind which the Germans had cleverly concealed a miniature anti-tank gun. This gun had managed to knock a track off the Sherman and check our progress, though I could not understand why the tank crew had failed to reply with their 76 mm gun.

A head cautiously appeared from the tank's turret and we called to him:

'In here tankie, over here.' The man saw us and spoke into the tank. Then the crew came out, sprinting for the house we occupied. We could hear the tank men downstairs discussing the situation. Their mate Ginger was still in the tank, wounded and unable to move.

'We'd better get him out somehow,' I heard one say.

'Come up here tankie,' called Sergeant Baxter, who had followed our section into the house. The crew joined us and the sergeant put them in the picture.

'We have a good view here,' he said. 'We can cover—.' Incredibly a German peered round the corner of the house opposite and Sergeant Baxter broke off in mid-sentence, stuck his Sten out of the window and fired a long burst. Brick splinters flew from the wall a couple of feet above the German's head and showered him.

'Missed the bastard,' said the sergeant as the German darted back. 'As I was saying, we can cover you from here,' he continued, turning again to the tank men as though the interruption had been a minor detail. The crew looked apprehensive, but retraced their steps to rescue Ginger. With encouragement from us they reached the disabled tank, carefully lifted out their mate and he was stretchered away.

We still had the final section of village to capture and the ice-cool, experienced Sergeant Baxter now took over.

'Right, Whitey,' he said, 'put a bomb through the window

over there, across that patch of wasteland, then you and Beachy
stay here and cover us while we run for it.' (Beachy's spell on the
mortar was short-lived; he had pushed the cumbersome weapon
onto one of the newcomers.) I sent a Piat bomb through the
upstairs window as directed and the blast was colossal, flushing
out three Germans who came running across the wasteland
towards us, holding their hands aloft. Sergeant Baxter and two
others went downstairs and dragged the prisoners into the
house. We were joined by another section and our sergeant
explained to them how Beachy and I would cover them while
they dashed across the open.

'Hey Fritz,' said the sergeant to one of the prisoners, 'your
Kameraden in *das Haus?*' He pointed to a house and shook his
Sten at the worried German.

'*Nein Kameraden,*' was the sullen answer. He had no
comrades in the house. The prisoners were looking decidedly
shaky; in the few minutes they had been with us our lads had
already ransacked their pockets.

'Right, follow me lads,' said the sergeant. 'Run like bloody
hell.' They had barely reached half-way across the wasteland
when automatic fire felled two lads from the other section and
the rest of the party, caught in the open and not knowing from
where the shots had come, doubled back to the house. They
crashed through the back door, breathless and wild-eyed.
Sergeant Baxter, gasping for air, took the stairs three at a time
and confronted Beachy and me.

'Where the bloody hell did that shooting come from?' he
demanded.

'Christ knows Sarge,' said Beachy. 'From the left, I think.
They still haven't cleared that big house over there.' The house,
about 200 yards to our left, was a solitary building in its own
grounds with an all-round field of fire.

Through our window we could see the two wounded lads
lying in the open, feebly waving to us. Sergeant Baxter,
concerned for them, now planned their rescue, with the help of
the corporal and four lads from the other section. Once again
the party moved out and reached the casualties without mishap.
The four lads lifted one of the wounded and slowly carried him
back to us while the two NCOs attended his mate. Sergeant
Baxter stood up to retrieve his field dressing from its pocket
when a single shot knocked him backwards. The corporal

looked about him helplessly for the briefest of moments and then raced back to the house, joining us upstairs. He was fuming and poked his Sten in our prisoners' faces.

'You bastards are coming out there with us,' he snarled, 'and if any of your bloody pals fire on us – you're dead.' Whether the Germans understood English or not the look on the corporal's face said it all. They had witnessed the shooting of Sergeant Baxter and must have felt ashamed.

Our platoon officer now arrived to enquire about the hold-up and after the corporal had explained the situation he agreed to use the prisoners to help rescue our two wounded mates. Accordingly the lieutenant sent his runner back for two stretcher-bearer teams and within minutes they had arrived and the plan was put into action.

Beachy and I, stationed at the upper window and keeping alert for enemy activity, especially from the large house on the left, watched the procession set out. First went a prisoner with hands held high, followed by the two other prisoners carrying a stretcher. Then came our medics, just to their right, thereby keeping the Germans between themselves and any snipers on the left. All went well and they recovered the wounded private, who had been hit in the legs. The operation was repeated, using the prisoners as shields again, and Sergeant Baxter was brought in. He seemed in a bad way, shot through the lung, with blood and froth coming from his lips when he tried to talk. I never learned whether the sergeant pulled through, but he was yet another veteran – one of the best – to fall by the wayside. Slowly and methodically the platoon's old, seasoned campaigners were being whittled away until only a handful remained. There was more bad news to come. Major Bob Anderson, our beloved company commander, was shot in the chest and critically wounded while leading an attack on nearby houses. He was invalided home, finishing the war with an OBE and a Military Cross and Bar.

Our Bren carriers now came to support us and did excellent work, charging about and helping us winkle out the few remaining defenders, stubborn to the end. It was a great feeling to have the village behind us and to receive the order, 'Dig in here, the Argylls are coming through.' Our sister battalion was always a welcome sight, despite their perennial sarcastic remarks about delays and hold-ups and leaving them to do all the hard grind.

No sooner had we finished our 'slitters' than the Argylls started to pass through, just as a short but accurate enemy artillery barrage arrived. Beachy and I, sharing a 'slitter', saw a blur of khaki and an Argyll thudded on top of us.

'That was bloody close,' said the new arrival, pushing his helmet from over his eyes to reveal wisps of red hair. His accent was pure joy to my ears – Black Country and beautiful. I looked at him, unable to believe my eyes. It was my good mate Billy Berridge, who lived close to me. We had grown up together.

'Bloody hell, Bill, fancy seeing you here,' I gasped.

'Well I'll be blowed, Stan,' he grinned. 'Bit of a bastard this, ain't it? How are you, old son?'

'I could be better,' I joked. 'I could be playing cricket on Cronehill's field' (referring to our local sports venue and my school playing fields). Billy looked wistful.

'Oh, ar, that'd be nice, eh?' he said. Peering over the top of the 'slitter' he gathered himself together.

'The lads are off. I'd better be moving Stan.' We shook hands and looked into each other's eyes; it was a look that spoke volumes, more meaningful than mere words. Billy heaved himself out of the 'slitter' and in the customary 'infantryman's crouch' ran forward to catch up with his mates.

'We'll try and meet up again, eh Bill?' I called after him. He turned round, wearing a broad grin.

'Let's bloody hope so mate,' he answered. 'See yer Stan.' Watching him trot forward I felt pangs of doubt and despair and wondered whether we would ever see each other again.

'There must be a million "slitters" in this here war and Billy has to land in mine,' I said to Beachy.

'What is known as the long arm of coincidence,' said my mate. Something tugged at my heartstrings as I recalled with a deep yearning those innocent, carefree, prewar days when Billy and I and other pals played cricket and football on our local playing fields. (Strangely enough, during my army service I was to meet five boyhood pals, all living within a stone's throw of me, which must have been something of a record.)

A nearby explosion roused me from my reverie. The sounds up front denoted that the Argylls were finding the going rough, and I fervently hoped that Billy would come through unharmed. I heard the call for stretcher-bearers and soon a Red Cross Jeep pulled up alongside us. These nippy little vehicles had been cleverly rigged to carry four stretchers and could venture close in to get the wounded away quickly.

Four stretcher-bearers jumped down and snatching two stretchers hurried towards the shouts. Soon they were struggling back with a casualty on each stretcher. Now a wounded man on a stretcher is no easy weight for two comrades to carry, and a dead man – who is literally dead weight – is an even greater burden, requiring someone on each corner. Seeing the lads labouring through the smoke with their cumbersome loads Beachy and I left our trench and rushed to lend a hand. While helping with the second casualty I felt a sudden shock as I looked down and saw a mop of red hair above the muddy, bloodstained face. It was my mate Billy Berridge. His face, always pale against his red hair, looked deathly white now and his eyes were closed. I was too shocked to say anything, as was Beachy; we merely shook our heads in disbelief.

The Jeep roared off and was crossing the waste ground we had fought over earlier when a heavy mortar barrage crashed down, obliterating the whole scene with dust and debris.

'Well I'll be buggered!' said Beachy. His blasphemous vocabulary was limited at the best, or rather the worst of times, but in my fury and anger I compensated.

'The lousy fucking bastards! Fancy mortaring a bloody Red Cross Jeep.'

'He was never meant to leave this spot alive, d'you think, Whitey?' said my mate disconsolately.

'Seems not. Poor Billy – copped it twice in ten minutes, and to think we were chatting here such a short while ago.' I felt very depressed.

At this point I must jump forward a couple of years and more to my demob leave back in England. While strolling through West Bromwich's Dartmouth Park, deploring its neglected, run-down state, I headed towards the lake bordering the park and saw someone approaching. He was rather bent forward and walked slowly, hesitantly. I'll have a chat with this old soul before returning home, I thought. Maybe I can cheer him up a little. He was looking at the ground, obviously deep in thought. As we came abreast I said 'Good morning' in a quiet voice, not wishing to startle him. He looked up and we both stood wide-eyed, mouths open. It was Billy Berridge.

'Bloody hell Stan!' he exclaimed. For a moment I was speechless and could feel the tears welling up. Our hands became locked in a firm clasp.

'Bloody hell Billy,' I finally blurted out, 'I thought you were killed at Waspik. I put you on a Jeep and then the bastards blew it up.'

'So I believe,' he grinned, 'but I don't remember much about it. I copped some shrapnel in the guts when I was on the Jeep, though the other bloke sort of shielded me. He copped the lot, poor bugger – and the driver too, apparently. I guess I was lucky, eh?'

'D'you fancy a drink and a chat?' I asked.

'I'd love to Stan, but I'm not allowed to drink. They've taken half my guts away and bits of shrapnel still work themselves out.'

'Well let's walk and talk,' I suggested. And so we had a pleasant tête-à-tête as we ambled round the park, each of us trying to cram four and more years' events into a few minutes. But it was pitiful to see the once active, virile, happy-go-lucky Billy now reduced to a stooping, halting invalid, living on a miserable disability pension. And yet Billy, big-hearted lad that he was, could only think of the lads he reckoned had returned from the war in a worse plight.

'Anyway, I'm glad you came through unscathed, Stan,' he said with feeling. Unscathed, I thought as we walked along. I did not have the heart to tell Billy that since returning from the European battlefields my nerves had been in tatters. 'Flashbacks' of war vividly sprang to life when triggered by something quite innocuous in everyday life – perhaps a tune on the bagpipes – that set me sweating and shaking violently; and I imagined that every bush and every nook hid a well-camouflaged Spandau nest. At night I suffered the most horrible and realistic nightmares, waking up lathered in sweat and shouting hysterically. For years afterwards I was unable to shake off the terror and the fear that stalked my waking hours and haunted my sleep, but I could not bring myself to burden Billy with my personal problems.

We reached the park gates, where our paths diverged, and shook hands cordially, promising to meet up again. As I watched my schoolboy pal wending his way slowly down the road I had a passionate longing for the days that used to be, before the war shattered so many young, lusty lives.

Back at Waspik, our unit was able to relax a little after the

Argylls had gone through and as we wandered back through the village we relived the battle, marvelling at the minute German anti-tank gun that had knocked out our Sherman, and its flimsy but effective camouflage of greenery. We inspected our disabled tank and studied the dead German lying nearby whom Shorty had dropped with three bullets in the throat. It was evident that someone had already rifled his pockets, leaving a wallet and personal papers on his chest. Shorty was annoyed at this infringement of the dead man's privacy and bent down to straighten the papers and stuff them back in the pockets. While doing so he noticed some family photos – evidently the man's wife and children and his parents – and was deeply affected as he realized the family's great loss. His shoulders began to shake and despite his valiant efforts to hide his feelings from the civilian onlookers now gathering, he sobbed and tears coursed down his cheeks. As he wept he cursed and groaned; cursed at the system that had made him kill this family man, and groaned at the suffering the relatives would endure. Corporal Grainger rebuked him for his self-reproach.

'The bugger was coming for you man. He wouldna be crying if it was the other way roond. Ah'm sure o' that.' We all agreed vociferously, whereupon Shorty gradually pulled himself together. But that was my mate Shorty MM, as we now called him: kind and thoughtful and sensitive. Before leaving we laid the dead German near the anti-tank gun, where our Pioneer boys would attend to him.

On a wild and windy night in November the 51st Highland Division took over from the 50th Northumbrian Division on Elst Island, a large area five or six miles west of the Dutch-German border, between Nijmegen and Arnhem, where the Rhine divides into two channels. Nijmegen Bridge, captured during the Market Garden operation by the combined efforts of the British Guards Armoured and American paras, linked the island to the city of Nijmegen.

Our first day was spent discreetly slipping back from the island into Nijmegen in covered trucks, disembarking in a side street, and boldly marching across the bridge back to the island. We continued this throughout the day, making a trip almost every hour. It was done simply to give the enemy the impression that the area was more heavily manned than was in fact the case.

The Germans, who controlled the Rhine sluices, had opened the floodgates and submerged the whole area, except for the main road and isolated farmsteads, which the locals had built well above sea level. We learned that animals on the scattered farms were starving and cows urgently needed milking, and in an effort to alleviate their suffering some of us set out on a mission of mercy. As the only means across the countryside was by boat, we had to ferry from one farmstead to another, using entrenching spades as paddles.

Lieutenant Robinson, an ex-para officer, had succeeded Lieutenant Bernard as our platoon officer, the latter having been slightly wounded by one of those accursed snipers. Robbo, as we called him, became restless at our non-military activities and decided to organize a patrol. He chose a 'farmhouse island' way out in no man's land, where he thought we should hole up at dusk, remain all the next day observing and return to base after dusk the same day.

'You'll come, won't you, Whitey? I'm looking for volunteers,' he said pointedly.

'I'd like to see who else is going first, sir,' I said, stalling. He secured eight 'volunteers' by going round saying he only required two more to make up the number, when in fact he had no names at all. None of us was able to verify his statements because we were so widely scattered on 'island farms'.

We had a trial run in our boat on the day of the patrol, the lieutenant kneeling in the boat's prow with a Bren and four of us each side paddling with spades. Our boat became stuck on an underwater obstacle and no amount of rocking or poking below the surface could free us. Then someone lowered his spade shaft to the bottom, which showed that the water was quite shallow.

'Oh, it's only a couple of feet deep, sir,' he called out.

'Right,' said our officer, 'I'll jump in and drag us clear.' So saying he grabbed the rope attached to the bows and slipped over the side. Sure enough, the water was shallow and the lieutenant was able to pull us free. As he stepped aside to let the boat glide by he disappeared underwater. When he surfaced, splashing and spluttering, we were too helpless with laughter to help him back into the boat. Luckily he had a sense of humour and after recovering his equilibrium was able to join in the laughter.

We returned to our respective sections to await, with some trepidation, the evening's patrol. For several days I had been suffering from earache and visited the RAP for cotton wool to stem the oozing fluid, not wanting to be in too much discomfort during the night-and-day patrol. The RAP orderly was reluctant to mess about with my ear.

'I'll have to send for the MO,' he said. 'The trouble is, he's at a piss-up down the road and won't be very pleased to be called away.'

'Well I can't go on patrol with my ear like this,' I insisted.

'Right, I'll ring him, but I wouldn't like to be in your shoes when he gets here.' The orderly wound the handle of the old field phone and after a brief conversation informed me that the MO would see me soon. I had not long to wait. The door crashed open and when I saw the MO's face, whisky flushed, with eyes raging, I knew I was in for it.

'What the bloody hell d'you mean, you can't go on patrol with earache?' he bellowed. 'Let's have a look at it.' He swabbed my ear and powdered it – none too gently – and left some cottonwool in it, all the while breathing his sickly-sweet whisky fumes in my face.

'Give me some spare cottonwool,' he said to the orderly, 'and have you got a red pen?' My good ear pricked up when he asked for a red pen. He intended giving me a 'Medicine and Duties' sick note in red ink, signifying that I was a scrounger and a malingerer. I had not heard of a red ink note since poor Ginger Thompson's time of torment two years earlier in Scotland.

'You drunken old bugger, you're not pulling that one on me,' I muttered to myself.

'Excuse me sir,' I said as he ripped a note off the pad, 'I know what MD [Medicine and Duties] red ink means. Before you write it would you please phone Lieutenant Robinson in B Company. He'll confirm that this is a volunteer patrol. I don't want to dodge it, I just want to be free from ear trouble while I'm out there. We'll be away a night and a day.'

'Ring B Company and ask for Lieutenant Robinson,' the MO snapped at the orderly. The orderly duly got through to our platoon officer and handed the phone to the MO.

'There's a chap here, Whitehouse, due out on a patrol. He's here with earache. Says he volunteered … Oh, I see, well, he'll be back in ten minutes.' The MO slammed the phone down and scribbled out my sick note – in blue ink.

'Here,' he snarled at me, passing the note, 'get one of your mates to swab the ear out, and squirt some of this powder in it every couple of hours.' I was reluctant to thank him, but did so half-heartedly. As I was leaving I gave the MO a quick hard look that was intended to say 'Prat'. I think he got the message.

Back with the platoon, we were preparing to set out when word came through from battalion that our patrol was cancelled. The CO could see no useful purpose in sending us out and felt it was not worth the risk. We eight 'volunteers' wholeheartedly concurred.

8   Near to Breaking Point

About this time I began to experience more acute symptoms of 'bomb happiness', or 'shell shock' as it was called in the earlier Great War. I had been in the line now, almost continuously, for more than six months and as week succeeded week I was having to dig deeper and deeper into those innermost resources of resolution, endurance and zeal to combat the gnawing, nagging fearfulness that filled my waking, and often sleeping, hours. As the campaign progressed I came to realize that for all the enemy's skill and doggedness he was more easily overcome than my troubled, tortured mind. I had long since forsaken that spirit of adventure, that devil-may-care attitude that had sustained me in the early days, when mates all around me were being killed and horribly maimed, and the whiplash of the murderous Spandau and the crunch of the mortars had men quivering in the bottom of their 'slitters'.

A newcomer to the platoon threw his mess tins down behind me and on hearing the clatter I flung myself down with undignified haste. The newcomer found it highly amusing, laughing loudly, whereupon I threatened to punch him on the nose, which was wholly unreasonable of me. But I was feeling generally irritable and peevish, ready to snap and snarl at the slightest provocation. And I was angry that I had lost my nerve while the replacements remained bold, and ashamed of my image in their eyes, a situation I was unable to rectify.

At the ripe age of eighteen and a few weeks I regarded myself as a veteran, doing nothing rash or heroic, supremely intent on survival, if only for a few more hours, a few more minutes. The perpetual, heartfelt cry 'When are we going to get a bloody break, Monty?' would go up from the trenches as many of us sank into a morbid state of mind. Although we were not aware at the time casualties and sickness among the infantry had been so heavy that few men could be spared for leave. After more than five years of war the country was nearing the bottom of the barrel in manpower, and while replacements were trickling in they generally lacked experience and know-how. These men, having grown accustomed to the good times in the rear, were finding life at the sharp end doubly tough.

A couple of our lads went 'on the trot' and as usual they were newcomers. So far we older hands – apart from Banger Brown – had resisted the temptation to desert; no doubt the harsh treatment meted out to Banger had deterred others from following his example. Another lad shot himself in the foot (an SIW – self-inflicted wound), or he thought he had. We heard the bang, followed by screams as he lay writhing on the ground.

'Oh God, me foot, me foot,' he cried, insisting that the gun had gone off accidentally. We dashed over, and while several of us held him, someone took off his boot and sock. The Sten bullet had passed between his big toe and the next one, merely grazing both. Stretcher-bearer Sergeant Tom King, that man of great understanding, and now the proud holder of the Military Medal, chuckled as he stuck a couple of plasters on the afflicted lad's toes.

'A bit of hard luck ye're havin' laddie, but we'll say nae mair aboot it, eh?' However, it set my mind working.

'It won't be long before I do something desperate,' I confided to my close pal Beachy.

'I know just how you feel,' he nodded wearily. Because of its fine spring and a heavy block, the Sten gun was notorious for being accidentally fired. Truck drivers in Normandy had been killed when jumping from their vehicles while carrying a Sten, the jerk of their arm on landing setting off the gun and catching them in the head. At the time it was thought snipers were responsible, and only when the death toll mounted was a closer examination made. Surprisingly the Sten had no safety catch, and though a crude safety mechanism was later fitted, our models were not modified.

I was feeling desperately washed out, unable to concentrate on anything except how to free myself from this nightmare existence and I finally summoned up the courage to engineer an 'accident' with the temperamental Sten. It certainly needed courage because first, if things went wrong I could be badly maimed for life; and second, if the truth were discovered I would be court-martialled, with all the consequences that entailed.

We were occupying an old farmhouse overlooking no man's land when I found myself alone in one of the rooms. I tested the mechanism of the Sten by taking off the magazine and banging the butt on the floor. The bolt shot up and down again, just as I had hoped. My cover story was that I had been hanging the Sten up by its sling when it slipped and as I went to grab it the butt hit the floor and it went off. I decided to aim for my hand and wrapped a field dressing round it to hide any powder burns.

I was alone in the room and a tremendous wave of relief swept over me as I took hold of the magazine to clip it on. Within seconds I would be free, free from the torment, the despondency and the apprehensions that dominated my mind. Suddenly the door opened and young Butler entered. I say young, though he was a little older than me, but he had been with us only a month or so and was young in experience, with an exuberance and energy that knew no bounds. When we were in action he was never far from me and in fact I had learned from one or two other lads that he idolized me. I must confess I liked him too and tried to teach him some of the finer points of infantry work, picked up the hard way coming through north-west Europe. But the sight of the youngster now, intruding upon my well-laid plans, filled me with anger and frustration. Had he been one of the old hands I would have said: 'Stand by matey, I'm trying for out', and I would no doubt have attempted an SIW. With Butler it was different. He was innocent and unknowing, still sharp and unwearied after a month of front line life, and knowing how he felt about me I did not have the heart to shatter his illusions. I felt ashamed at the vast difference in our attitudes: whereas he was zealous and aglow with the thrill of it all I hid my fears behind a façade.

The youngster breezed into the room, smiling broadly.

'Hiya Stan. What's up with your hand?' he asked with concern, looking down at the field dressing.

'Oh it's nothing Butt. I just caught it on some bleedin' wire,' I said, trying to make light of it.

'There's a couple of Jerries mooching about in front of our positions. Shall we see what they're up to?' he asked excitedly. 'They don't seem to be carrying weapons.'

Dismissing thoughts of an SIW, I took the Sten and Butler carried his rifle as we set out to investigate. The two men, in bluish-grey uniforms, were in no man's land, slowly coming our way. They waved and we levelled our weapons at them to show we meant business. As they drew near one called out in pure Oxford English:

'It's all right old boy, we're just after a few souvenirs.' Then I noticed their uniforms; they were RAF chaps, sporting pilot's wings. I was livid.

'You'd better get over here bloody fast,' I yelled. 'We're liable to shoot anything out there.' They came over, quite unconcerned, and said they flew Typhoons and had taken a Jeep ride to the front to collect mementoes.

'Bloody idiots,' said my protégé after the airmen had left. 'It would have served the buggers right if we'd shot 'em.'

Unexpectedly I had temporary relief from my abysmal, despairing state of mind. With the campaign now well under way and battalion HQ more organized, a scheme was arranged whereby one man from each platoon – four in all – was sent to join B echelon, a mile or two back from the front line, for two or three days. With almost forty men to a platoon these spells out of the line were very infrequent and when my turn came to move back I was ecstatic.

That mile or two to the rear was as good as a hundred or two hundred to front-liners perpetually on the *qui vive*. To be able to walk upright instead of hurrying around in that hunched up trot was heavenly; and sleeping prone instead of in a sitting position at the bottom of a cold, damp hole, with your mate's muddy boots treading over you as he wriggled to try and ease his cramped legs was sheer bliss. Above all, to be under a roof and dry, even when it rained, was sublime.

We chosen four joined B echelon stalwarts – cooks, clerks, storemen, tailors and so on, who were mostly ex-Desert Rats – in a clean barn with neatly laid-out bedrolls. But we sensed an unbridgeable gap between us. They were appreciably older and seemed embarrassed and uneasy because we were members of the front-liners' club – 'the most exclusive club in the world', as one famous general described it – and to hide their feelings they dwelt at length on their days in the Western Desert. But as Geordie Barnes (Barney), one of our quartet told them: 'It's us wee bairns that's doin' the scrappin', not ye.' A hundred yards behind the front line and you were not 'in the club'. A strange state of affairs in an infantry battalion, but that is how it was.

We four gathered together at our own end of the barn, built a little 'stockade' with bales of straw and settled down to sleep, yarn, write letters, eat and sleep again. Geordie Barnes made his mark on our first day with B echelon. He was a reinforcement to us from the Tyneside Scottish Battalion, and he came bounding into our 'stockade' that first night wearing a huge grin.

'Look what ah've found chaps.' He opened his blouse to reveal two bottles of whisky nestling inside.

'Where did they come from?' I asked.

'Ah, dinna worry, Whitey, there's bloody stacks of it back there.' Senior NCOs got a monthly whisky and rum allowance and if any were killed their allowance continued. We slept the sleep of the dead that night – courtesy of Johnny Walker.

I was rudely awoken by Barney shouting and banging his boots, then jumping from bale to bale, his shirt tails flapping.

'What's goin' on, you noisy swine?' demanded Chuck Bowyer, another of our quartet.

'Twa moose, twa moose – in ma twa bits,' shouted Barney, almost hysterically.

'What the hell's he saying?' I asked.

'He's got two mice in his boots,' translated Chuck.

'I thought they had him by the balls the way he was hollering,' said our fourth buddy, Eddie Ward.

Our second day was spent generally relaxing again, showering, writing, dozing. In the evening we had bread and cheese and a mug of cocoa, liberally laced with whisky, though Barney reckoned his was a mug of whisky with a dash of cocoa. The liquor soon loosened our tongues and Barney especially was in fine form, relating a tale about his days with the Tyneside Scottish.

'We were out of the line for a few days,' he began, 'and me and my mate were sent to B echelon to dig a slit-latrine as punishment for not cleaning the Bren properly.' He paused for a swig from his mug. 'We'd finished digging the bloody new trench when the RSM comes along and tells us to cart the soil from the new latrine and tip it into the one the men had been using – about ten yards away. We'd tipped one load out and were sitting on the barrow having a smoke when we heard a helluva clatter and machine-gunning. Then over a hedge swooped a Jerry plane, all guns blazing.' He took another drink and we followed suit.

'Well, me and my mate looked at each other for less than a split second and dived into the filthy, bloody, smelly trench.' He was unable to continue for laughing and we all joined in. 'Ah'm sure me mate shit himself,' he finally continued. 'Ah know ah nearly did, and it took me weeks to get rid of the awful pong.'

The talk somehow veered round to marriage, and Chuck Bowyer held our attention.

'I think I might be hitched,' he said, 'but then again I'm not sure.'

'What the hell's that supposed to mean?' I asked.

'Well, just before we were penned in for D-Day I was paralytic drunk and had a great time with a local lass. Anyway, after that she got a special marriage licence because she said I'd put her in the family way and I was going abroad. I vaguely remember bits of the wedding ceremony and her putting me on the train back to barracks. She is now my next of kin and entitled to a marriage allowance and a pension if I cops it. But it seems she wasn't pregnant at all and married me under false pretences.'

'I'm surprised you fell for that one,' laughed Eddie.

'Which one's that?' I asked intrigued.

'Some of these girls are getting hold of forged special marriage licence permits,' explained Eddie. 'Then they give a squaddie a good time for a day or two, getting him drunk and then hitched. Like Chuck says, they've got an allowance and if he cops it they get a pension.'

'Yeah, and doin' it more than once,' snorted Chuck. 'Just before D-Day I had a letter from my folks saying my bint was a prozzy on the game, marrying any bugger she could get her claws into, using different names for herself. God knows what number I am on her list. Anyway,' he concluded, 'my folks are sorting it out, although, come to think of it, she was a nice ride.'

Later, when the whisky was beginning to liven up the party, making us boisterous and even more talkative, a big fellow I knew sauntered over. We called him Big Jim, the company HQ radio man, and I admired him tremendously. He ran radio lines between company HQ and platoons and was quite fearless, taking his lines where possible 'as the crow flies', which sometimes meant venturing into areas we had not fully cleared. Whereas the other wire men worked in pairs, taking longer but safer routes, Big Jim preferred working alone and had already been slightly wounded four times. He was a tall, well-built, fair-haired Cockney who reminded me of the Tarzan actor Johnny Wiessmuller.

'Tell the lads about your first "wound", Jim,' I said, seeing his grinning face appear over the bales of straw. He looked a little sheepish.

'I don't know whether I should,' he said. 'But if you insist. I was laying wires at a farmhouse, keeping the lines high so they wouldn't snag anything. There was me up a ladder hammering a nail next to an upper window when a smashin' *mademoiselle* opened the window. I thought she was going to tell me off for the noise, but with a nice smile, a nod and a wink she pulled me through the window into her room.' Four pairs of eyes were riveted on Big Jim, hanging on his every word as the spicy tale began to unfold.

'Before I knew it we were in bed having a right old time. Suddenly we heard heavy footsteps downstairs.

' "Shhhh," whispered my bedmate, putting a finger to her gorgeous lips. Then someone began climbing the stairs and the crafty bitch started hitting me and yelling: *"Papa, papa! Vite! Vite!"* I realized what the scheming little bugger was up to. If papa catches us at it she's in the clear if she shouts "Rape". I was out of that window in a flash, I can tell you. But I fell off the bloody ladder half way down and badly hurt my arm, though I didn't dare stop in case papa had a shotgun. It turned out I'd fractured my arm and was in hospital for a couple of weeks eyeing up the nurses. I think I was company HQ's first casualty – "fractured in action", I suppose,' he chuckled.

'By the way lads,' he said, adopting a more serious tone, 'I hear D Company caught a pasting last night. A Jerry patrol got through and shot 'em up. Four blokes copped it, and they nabbed a lance-corporal. The CO's bloody fuming, because D Company were in reserve positions, almost resting.'

'The cunning buggers knew what they were doing,' I chipped in. 'When you're in reserve you tend to leave it to the front-liners. The poor sods from D must have wondered what hit them.' As I swallowed I felt my throat tighten and the palms of my hands became sticky with sweat. I was mollified somewhat on noticing that my mates' faces suggested that they too were affected by Big Jim's bad news. Here in the comparative safety of the barn I felt guilty at the thought of my mates up the road being killed. Dwelling further on the matter, a cold fear seemed to creep all over me – the fear that caused men to smash their trigger finger with a mess-tin full of sand, rub dust into open sores, put a bullet in their foot, or even feign madness. It was the fear of being hideously disfigured or mutilated, the fear of letting my mates see I was so petrified that I could not think or act rationally. And of course there was the fear of death, of being robbed of a life only half lived, with so much more living and loving, happiness and laughter still to come. Fear was indeed a stout opponent if you were a combatant in the front line. It seemed that even among B echelon I could not shake off these sinister thoughts.

Big Jim, realizing that he had put a damper on our roistering, laughingly cadged another generous helping of whisky.

'Must go chaps,' he said, downing the whisky. 'Gotta pull me wire. Ha-ha-ha!' And he left us.

Someone wondered what we would all do back home after the war, when it was all over. It may have been the whisky talking, but the general consensus, as voiced by Chuck was: 'Let's get through it first. It's no good making plans if we don't make it.'

To look ahead just a little, Chuck Bowyer certainly survived the fighting, though I noticed a gradual change in his personality, so that by the end of the war he was no longer the happy-go-lucky, easy-going squaddie sharing our laughs and frolics in that dilapidated barn.

Soon after the war, when the Black Watch had gone home and we were transferred to the Lincolnshire Regiment in the small German town of Gevelsburg, we met Paddy Lawson, a thoroughly evil man. He had joined the Lincolns after being released from a POW camp and wore a huge chip on his shoulder, determined to seek revenge on the Germans for the hardships he had endured behind barbed wire. He and his small gang – two of whom had also been POWs – terrorized the locals, robbing and beating them indiscriminately and generally making life very unpleasant for the folk of that little town. Unfortunately Chuck Bowyer fell under Lawson's spell and joined in with equal gusto as the gang burgled houses every night and lurked in dark alleys to pounce on anyone still about. At the time a curfew was in force and Paddy and Chuck and the others used this as an excuse to waylay and rob people walking the streets after dark.

The rest of us tolerated this outrageous behaviour only because Paddy insisted that the Germans had shown him and his mates no mercy during their captivity. But now that the fighting had ceased the British Army was trying to improve relations with our former enemies in an effort to restore some sort of order from the utter chaos reigning in Germany.

One night Paddy and Chuck, who had built up an unenviable reputation among the townsfolk for brutality, set about a lone German in a side-street and realized they had walked into a trap when about a dozen big, brawny men fell upon them. Paddy was an all-action boxer who had beaten all comers (including me) but he and Chuck were no match for these avenging Germans, who left the pair bloodied, bruised and in hospital. Most of us were delighted to learn that Paddy in particular had received a dose of his own medicine, but unfortunately the matter did not rest there. Paddy was hell-bent on retribution.

One night he accosted a courting couple in a quiet lane on the outskirts of town and insisted the girl go with him. When her young man protested Paddy pulled out a pistol and shot him dead. At an identity parade involving the whole battalion the distraught young *Fräulein* picked out Paddy three separate times, but the sadist had a perfect alibi: he was in hospital at the time of the shooting. Chuck Bowyer, also a hospital patient, vouched for Lawson and he was acquitted, though most of us were convinced of his guilt. Every squaddie knew that the back door of a military hospital saw far more comings and goings than the main entrance, and it would have been easy for Paddy to slip out unnoticed and return after the murder.

Soon afterwards Paddy was due for demobilization and he and his cronies had a farewell drink in the canteen, where several of us gathered in case any fun developed. With the *Schnaps* flowing freely Chuck bragged openly of having saved his hero from a life sentence for the killing. Even Paddy boasted of the vengeance he had wreaked on the young German for his beating up. Those of us who heard confirmation of what we strongly suspected were incensed but regrettably did nothing about it. The war had just finished and in this topsy-turvy, unreal world it was just another killing of a German by an Englishman. And Chuck, Lawson's accomplice, was equally guilty.

But all that was some way into the future. For now there was still a war to be won and Chuck – showing no hint of his future aggressive behaviour – enjoyed with us LOB (left out of battle) wallahs a few more precious hours of sleeping and lazing in our tumbledown barn before we had to report back to the line.

It was a prospect that filled me with foreboding. No doubt the rest was beneficial – to the mind more so than to the body perhaps – but soon it would be nothing more than an idyllic memory.

Christmas was just round the corner – a matter of days away – and we were hoping for something special in our rations, and maybe extra mail. The line had been extremely quiet and one or two of the more optimistic squaddies even ventured to suggest a spot of leave might be in the offing. Then unexpected news came through of a mighty German push further south in the wooded Ardennes region of Belgium and Luxembourg. We sensed that something big was afoot, but not until later did we learn the full extent of the enemy's thrust. Powerful Panzer and infantry divisions had been flung against a lightly-held American sector, with the ambitious aim of pushing right on to Antwerp, thereby splitting the Allied armies and possibly creating another Dunkirk. The ensuing Battle of the Bulge, as it became known because of the dent or bulge in the Allied line, was to prove a bitter and costly affair, and probably prolonged the war.

The 51st Highland Division, along with other units, became a temporary mobile force and was rushed south to help stem the enemy advance. We could say goodbye to any Yuletide festivities for the foreseeable future.

As we travelled south in trucks the drab, monotonous Dutch landscape was succeeded by more picturesque vistas of hills, woods and winding roads. Perhaps my most abiding memory of the Ardennes was the intense, bitterly cold weather. A biting wind blew from Siberia right across eastern Europe, bringing Arctic conditions of ice and snow and sub-zero temperatures – the most severe winter, apparently, for more than fifty years. Our personal weapons froze up and to cock a rifle we had to hammer the bolt in position with a piece of wood, a stone or any other handy object. We were issued with graphite grease to rub on the mechanism, but it too froze. The ground was frozen solid and with digging out of the question we sheltered in farmhouses or barns. So severe was the weather that sentries hugged garden walls and had to be relieved every twenty minutes.

On our first night we were driven up to the defensive front line the battered Americans were holding to relieve one of their companies. It was a beautiful, crisp, starlit night, with the frozen snow crunching under our feet, and as we waited in the shadow of tall, stately pines on the edge of a forest the vapour of our breath hung on the calm, frost-laden air.

Our platoon commander, Lieutenant Robinson, and his American counterpart met and casually exchanged salutes and shook hands before the American escorted our officer into the forest. Several minutes later a ragged column of about sixty GIs came shuffling towards us from the direction the officers had taken. Usually infantry units passing each other exchanged lively banter, but not on this occasion. The sullen GIs trudged wearily past us, faces swathed in scarves and balaclavas and buried in greatcoats.

'Into the trucks fellas,' were the only words I heard from the NCO who led them out. Once in their vehicles they sat hunched up and silent, a picture of utter despair. There were no sarcastic remarks from us; in the past we too had suffered severe setbacks and our hearts went out to them. The last man in the column, a sergeant, said softly:

'I'm told to contact Sergeant McKenzie.'

'That's me,' said our Sergeant Mac, stepping forward. They shook hands.

'Glad to see you guys,' said the American. 'Follow me.' We tagged behind in single file and came to what had obviously been a hunting lodge, made of logs and stone, surrounded by a four-foot dry stone wall. One part of the building was badly scorched and blackened, and there was a hole in the roof, but the lodge was habitable. The two sergeants stood looking over the glistening snow to their front.

'So where's Jerry from here?' asked Sergeant Mac.

'Gee Sarge, I truthfully don't know,' said the GI. 'My guys have been so shattered I couldn't ask them to shove out on patrols.' He pointed to the hole in the roof.

'The Krauts gave us that a couple of days ago, but it's been quiet since then.' His officer appeared and shook Mac's hand.

'Gotta go, the trucks are waiting,' he said. 'Good luck. Give the bastards one for us.' With a weary wave to us all they left and long after they had gone the crunch of their receding boots on the hard snow carried to us on the crisp night air.

Our lieutenant organized hot stew from our compo packs, supplemented by the excellent food our allies had left us. Sentries were posted around the perimeter walls, to be relieved at twenty-minute intervals, so that every man had several short sharp spells in that frigid, raw weather. The Americans also left spray cans of an anti-freeze weapon oil, which proved far more effective than our graphite grease. Trust the Yanks, with their vast resources, to have the answer.

The lodge's stone floor was surprisingly warm, which puzzled us, but we were too tired to give it more than a passing thought as we slumped down to sleep, only to be rudely kicked awake in the bleakest watches of the night for a short but agonizing spell of sentry duty in those Arctic conditions.

The next morning we solved the mystery of the warm stone floor. Outside the lodge a door led to a stone basement, half full of slow-burning logs. It was a crude but effective heating system, similar, I believe, to methods devised by the ancient Romans.

Later our old friend Lysander Lizzie cruised over the front line for about ten minutes before waggling her wings and returning to base. Soon afterwards a Jeep carrying our battalion commander came bouncing over the frozen ruts and slithered to a halt outside the lodge. Apparently, to our front, hidden by a copse, was a farmhouse which was assumed to be empty, but Lysander Lizzie had reported footprints in the surrounding virgin snow, causing a flap at battalion HQ.

'Could you have a look, old boy?' the CO asked our lieutenant.

'Yes sir, yes sir,' said the platoon commander, his face aglow at the prospect of action.

'Three bags fucking full sir,' muttered a wag warming his hands by the stove.

'Why don't they leave Jerry alone?' asked his mate. 'He ain't bothering us.'

'No, but he bleedin' well might tonight,' said Shorty.

After the CO had left, our officer and Sergeant Mac began planning the patrol while we all tried to make ourselves as inconspicuous as possible.

Lieutenant Robinson, a Birmingham lad, had been in the paras, but after breaking an ankle during the Normandy drop, which rendered him suspect for further jumps, he was posted to us. He was razor keen and expected us war-weary squaddies to do everything at the double. Nevertheless, he was popular and cared for his men. Now, as he and the sergeant planned the patrol, I overheard their talk.

'We might as well go prepared for trouble,' said the lieutenant, 'so I'll take two Bren men – er ... and the Piat man,' he added as an afterthought.

'Oh balls!' I muttered under my breath. 'Here we go again.'

'So it will be Head and Shorthouse Brens and Whitehouse Piat,' concluded Robbo quietly. Sergeant Mac looked round at us.

'D'yer hear that yous three? Be ready at dusk. OK?'

The moon, almost full, cast an ethereal glow over the whole ivory panorama as we set out for the spinney to our front. Crunching on the crisp snow was like wading through a myriad of diamonds that glistened and sparkled as they reflected the moon's brilliance.

On reaching the far edge of the pines we halted in the shadows and could clearly see the farm, about 120 yards away, with chinks of light at its windows.

'That's handy,' whispered Robbo, pointing to a stack of logs, half-buried in snow, midway between us and the farm. 'Let's get there and listen,' he added. We were soon out in the open, fully exposed, and wading through the snow with our heavy equipment was arduous. Nevertheless we reached the logs without mishap and flopped down, breathless.

'Put a bomb through the window, Whitey, and you two Brens shoot anything that comes out,' ordered our officer. I looked across at Shorty and sensed by his expression that he was as angry as me. We had been told to look and listen, not rashly tackle the unknown enemy. I set my sights for fifty yards and heard the Brens being cocked.

'OK Whitey?' asked the lieutenant.

'Hold it, hold it,' whispered Heady excitedly, 'they're coming out.' The door opened and the light from inside streamed out onto the snow. In its golden shaft we saw three small children come tumbling out, laughing and shouting, followed by a tiny yapping dog.

'Bugger me, that was close,' gasped Robbo, pushing his helmet back on his head.

'What now sir?' I asked. 'I don't think there's any Jerries in there.' A man and a woman came to the door, calling the children. Suddenly our officer stood up and waved his arms.

'Hello, hello, English here, English here,' he shouted. The children and their dog stopped in their tracks, then the dog approached, barking noisily. The couple in the doorway looked towards us and we all waved.

'Tommies,' I yelled.

'Ah, Tommies,' called the lady. 'Come, come, Tommy, *ney Mofferman*, Tommy, come.' I gave a huge sigh of relief at the news that there were no Germans in the vicinity. We went into the farmhouse and I felt like an intruder from another planet gatecrashing this little family's simple but cosy home that had so far escaped the ravages of war. Our officer asked the couple if they wished to return with us, and I was not surprised when they declined. They seemed content knowing that we were just a few fields away, and in any case they felt that this senseless war had nothing to do with them.

Later that night, back at the lodge, I awoke from a nightmare, shouting and sweating profusely. In my dream we were lying in the snow behind those logs aiming our weapons at the farmhouse. The door swung open and we all opened fire ....

We occupied La Roche village, littered with German corpses – presumably a result of our artillery shelling – and in the sub-zero temperature the bodies looked so fresh we thought they were still alive. After the village had been pounded by our big guns we were ordered to deal with SS men still holding out. We edged forward among the rubble, our boots sliding on the icy road, when an unknown British officer appeared in front and was promptly shot. As he crawled back an SS man boldly stood up, pulled the ring on a stick grenade and slithered it along the frozen ground. It came to rest against the crawling officer and exploded, killing him. No one had been able to fire on the German because our weapons were frozen up again.

The effervescent Lieutenant Robinson now took a hand.

'Come on, you dozy buggers, let's get moving,' he exhorted us, dancing on top of a heap of rubble.

'Snipers about sir, snipers,' several of us warned him.

'Snipers? There are no bloody snipers. Get up! Follow me!' Reluctantly we began to rise when a single shot rang out and Lieutenant Robinson rolled down the rubble heap to rest at our feet. He had been shot in the back, the bullet lodging in his chest.

Beachy and I, sheltered by the heap, unhitched his pack and placed our field dressings under his shirt on to the wound. But we realized this was useless; he needed urgent attention. First four of us, then six tried to lift him, but conditions underfoot were so slippery that we were unable to keep our feet. The lieutenant's pack was nearby and someone suggested using his groundsheet as a sort of sledge to slide him along the glassy surface. It worked well, though Lieutenant Robinson must have found it most uncomfortable and painful as we dragged him over the bumpy road. Nevertheless, he was soon at the RAP, receiving expert attention, though I never heard whether he survived his dreadful wound. We later looked over his pack and marvelled at the path of the bullet that felled him. It had entered his pack and travelled through mess tins and even bars of chocolate before finishing in his chest.

Once again we were without an officer. Platoon commanders were snipers' prime targets, a lesson we had soon learned in Normandy, but a new breed of officers coming through made the enemy sharpshooters' task so much easier by flaunting themselves in the front line with map boards, binoculars and other trappings of rank. Their bravery was never in question, but it was seldom tempered with prudence or circumspection. Some might just as well have strolled about in pink pyjamas. One evening earlier in the campaign we received a new officer who quickly visited each 'slitter', introducing himself and saying he would speak to us properly in the morning. We never saw him again. He rose at dawn to attend to his ablutions and became another sniper victim. Quite often our CSM or a senior sergeant acted as platoon leader while we awaited a replacement.

By mid-January the full weight of the Allied armies had blunted the enemy's Ardennes assault, though the Americans played by far the major role, suffering severe casualties. The bulge in our lines was pinched out and the 51st Highland Division withdrew to

Grave in Holland to prepare for a crack at the redoubtable Siegfried Line, the Germans' most fearsome bastion, guarding the Fatherland itself.

9   The Reichswald Forest

Shorty Shorthouse and I were regularly summoned to company HQ.

'Look you two,' the company commander would say, 'it's about time you took a tape apiece. We desperately need good, experienced men as NCOs. How about it?' We always refused. When first asked I was still only seventeen and had no intention of giving orders to a married man, probably with a family, and maybe getting him killed. Shorty's reason for refusing was a little more selfish:

'I've enough trouble keeping myself alive, without worrying about any other bugger,' he would say to me, though he phrased it a little more tactfully to the company commander. While at Grave, preparing for the assault on the Siegfried Line, we were sent for again and this time, before seeing the OC, we discussed the pros and cons of becoming junior NCOs. Of the 36–40 men in our platoon on D-Day only about ten remained and recent reinforcements seemed to be of poor quality. We learned from the general talk that the majority of newcomers had been living in comfortable camps, with showers and regular meal times, within hailing distance of the fleshpots of Brussels and Antwerp, places we only knew as dots on the map. Others had been winkled out of half-forgotten hidey-holes and sent to the pool of reserves, where all the infantry dross seemed to collect before being dispatched to short-handed units.

Most of these men had forgotten all the infantry tactics learned back home: how to dig in, camouflage, recognize minefields and boobies, and try to stay one step ahead of the well-trained, disciplined and conniving enemy. Coming up through France and Belgium I thought the standard of newcomers had generally deteriorated and invariably, after participating in an attack or a patrol, one or two went missing.

Looking around at the new reinforcements and not relishing the prospect of one of them being promoted and giving us orders, we decided to take a stripe. We thought it better for us to give the new lads the benefit of our hard-earned experience, rather than their learning the tricks of the trade at our expense. So, purely for selfish reasons – if one's survival can be called selfish – Shorty and I became lance-corporals. Being dogsbody to a platoon commander and half a dozen or so men in the section was an unpaid and often thankless job, but I quite enjoyed it. One of my tasks was to check that squaddies had sufficient ammunition and rations in their kit before going into battle. I also had to pair off pick and spade men. Newcomers were amazed to find that everyone carried either a full-sized pick or a spade into action. These life-saving tools were stuck in the belt between the ammunition pouches, and it was essential to team up a pick man with a spade man so that digging-in could be done quickly. If we had casualties the pairings had to be rearranged.

Now we were issued with a new instrument – a prodder, also carried in the belt. The Germans were sowing thousands of Schu mines, made of plywood and resembling cigar boxes, which, because of their wooden construction, could not be spotted by our conventional detectors. The prodders were merely four-foot metal rods with which we were supposed to prod the ground in front of us as we advanced.

We first encountered the Schu mines in Holland, quickly losing half a dozen men. They were cheap but formidable weapons, being triggered by the slightest tread and could easily remove a man's foot. As he fell sideways he often exploded another mine, which blew off a hand or an arm. Divisional HQ offered a two-week Blighty leave to anyone solving the Schu mine problem, but nothing had materialized, so we were stuck with the prodder. Flail tanks dealt with the mines easily enough, but were not always available.

It was asking a lot of a squaddie expecting him to go into action poking about with his prodder like a blind man, while at the same time keeping an eye on the enemy ahead and somehow having his personal weapon handy. I never saw the prodder being used and soon it was discarded altogether. Looking back, I marvel at the accoutrements we had to carry into battle. Even without the prodder, they must have weighed well in excess of 60 lb.

Early in February platoon officers were called to company HQ to receive orders for the attack on the Reichswald Forest, through which the Siegfried Line and the German frontier ran. Later, NCOs were put in the picture by Lieutenant Bernard, our platoon commander, now recovered after being wounded by a sniper. We gathered round a map spread out in front of us.

'This map has come from Intelligence,' said the lieutenant, 'and we have a specific job here.' He glanced up at our faces while tapping the map and could not have been inspired by our blank expressions.

'It doesn't look too difficult and they're giving us our own tank.' He looked up again, smiling. 'First we cross this open ground under smoke. Right? But we have to follow the tank that will be carrying two enormous bales of chestnut fencing, planks, ladders, duckboards – the lot.' Our frowns grew deeper and a little more bewilderment and apprehension registered in our eyes.

'Here, just on the edge of the forest,' explained Lieutenant Bernard, indicating a spot on the map, 'is a 23-feet-wide ditch. No depth is given, but we suspect it's a tank trap, and our tank will tip the bales of fencing into the ditch. But he won't continue, as the tanks can't make headway among the trees. So we have to unload the planks and duckboards quickly and make a bridge over the ditch for the Bren carriers to cross in support. Got it?'

'Sounds a bit bloody funny to me having a ditch so wide,' someone muttered.

'Well don't forget it's the start of the Siegfried Line,' said the lieutenant. 'We've got to expect anything now.' Our platoon commander concluded by saying that the attack would be preceded by a heavy barrage.

I was feeling jittery and out of sorts as I contemplated the morning's assault on the redoubtable Siegfried Line. An accumulation of events were taking their toll on my once-resilient frame of mind. Two young Jocks who had just joined us were singing 'Bonnie Scotland' and other popular Scottish songs when I rounded on them.

'Stop that bloody racket and give your voices a rest,' I snapped. They glared at me and I returned the glare.

'What's the matter with you?' asked one, yet another red-haired lad we called Ginger and so like my old buddy Ginger Thompson, killed on an exercise in Scotland. I knew I was out of order complaining about their singing. If they were happy I should let them sing all day long. But my nerves were as taut as piano wires and my stomach as heavy as lead. I glared even harder at them.

'See if you feel like singing this time tomorrow,' I snarled.

At dawn came the dreaded order 'get dressed', filling me with all the old worries and doubts – only a thousand times more pronounced. A tremendous and deafening barrage – one of the heaviest I could recall – went some way towards assuaging my worst fears as we headed for the start line. There is no doubt that an artillery barrage – and especially one of this vehemence – could act as a potent morale booster.

We were ordered to crawl through the initial scrubland while awaiting the smoke bombs and had barely started when the bombs rained down among us, instead of fifty to sixty yards ahead. Two or three fell within feet of me and I hugged the ground, paralysed with fear. How could they miss me? It was among the most terrifying experiences of my life. I considered crawling back but when one landed a couple of feet from my head I had to hide my face in my arms to breathe, as the black, choking stuff swirled all around me. After what seemed an eternity the bombing stopped, leaving me gasping for breath and rubbing my watery, stinging eyes.

'On your feet,' shouted Lieutenant Bernard. 'Keep behind this tank 6 Platoon.' We edged forward, tucked behind the Sherman, which looked strangely top-heavy with its giant load of bridging materials. As we passed taller scrub on our right there was a burst of gunfire and Little Mac, nearest the scrub, gave a shout and fell. The lieutenant looked over to me.

'Clear that scrub,' he ordered. I hesitated, feeling scared, and Shorty came to my rescue.

'I'll go Whitey. Follow me 9 Section.' My mate and his lads rushed through the scrub but found nothing. Poor Little Mac had been killed by our other platoon, who had fired into the scrub haphazardly from the far side of the patch.

There was a slight explosion nearby and Corporal Aitchison, only a few yards from me, crumpled in a heap. A Schu mine had blown off his foot. His Sten flew out of his hands and on landing set off another mine. Bastard things, I thought. But what should I do? If I ventured near Aitch to help him I could well become another mine victim. Aitch's anguished face turned to me and my heart went out to him.

'Stay back Stanley, stay back. I'll be OK,' he called, grimacing as he waved me away. (He was the only one who called me Stanley.) The corporal was a man I had always admired, but never more than now when he showed real courage and understanding as he sensed my dilemma.

'OK Aitch. See you pal,' I called. Fortunately our stretcher-bearers, cautiously prodding for more mines, soon reached the wounded corporal. The start line was still crowded, hence the stretcher-bearers' prompt arrival, and I noted ambulances chugging forward too, which was comforting.

We struggled on behind our tank as enemy shells and Spandaus continued their lethal work. I heard the bagpipes start up and thought the player would be more useful with a gun in his hand. As we neared the tree line an explosion behind was followed by cries and panicky shouting. Some of company HQ personnel had been hit by a shell, dropped short, we suspected, by our own artillery. The tank stopped and its commander popped his head out of the turret.

'Where's that bloody big ditch?' Lieutenant Bernard shouted to him.

'There's no sign of it here. It must be further in the forest,' replied the tank officer. 'But this is as far as I go,' he added. We rushed past the Sherman to the borderline trees and dropped into a handy little trench, about three feet wide, to await orders. Our platoon officer soon joined us.

'Company HQ's had a hit,' he said, with a note of urgency in his voice. 'It fell between the Bren and mortar men. Send someone back for the weapons Whitehouse. We can't leave them there. I'll go and see what's doing,' and scrambling out of the trench he went back towards company HQ. I turned to Private Ray Carpenter, one of the few remaining D-Day originals.

'Will you and Jock go back and get the Bren and mortar, Ray?' I asked.

He went white and burst into tears.

'For Christ's sake, Whitey, there's snipers out there. Please don't ask me to go.' Ray was constantly looking at photos of his wife and children and was probably in a worse mental state than me – hanging on by the slenderest of threads. I tried to be firm.

'Some bugger's got to go Ray.'

Now he played his ace:

'I've got a family – wife and kids, Whitey. Send one of the young 'uns.' There was a pleading, despairing look in his eyes. I glanced at the rest of the section and they all turned away, as though engrossed elsewhere.

'Come on Ginger, follow me,' I said, kicking Ginger's foot and setting out for the two bodies lying in the open, about fifty yards back. It was reassuring to see the follow-up troops coming towards us. When we reached the smouldering scene the shock took my breath away. I was horrified to see Ken Ware, eyes glazing over, his face creased with pain and his limbs shattered. Blood, a strange light brownish colour, was bubbling out of his legs. Larry Crowther, his best mate, lay nearby, in an equally hopeless condition. Ginger looked down and seemed to go into a trance. Struggling to combat nausea, I picked up the mortar and pushed it into Ginger's hands; then I scooped up the Bren and we hightailed it back to the cover of the trees. I pulled out a clump of long grass and wiped the worst of the blood and gore from the Bren. Ray Carpenter looked at me, eyes full of tormented questions.

'Ken Ware and Larry Crowther,' I said. Ray bit his lip and hid his face in the grass.

'Oh Christ!' I heard him sob quietly. I felt initial guilt at the way I had so hastily, almost irreverently, left Ken and Larry back there. But then I knew they would have understood that I could do nothing, exposed as I was to enemy fire. In any case, they were beyond help. Ken and Larry, two of the most gentle, lovable chaps ever born, now lay in bits and pieces. I had been particularly fond of Ken, who was with me at the crossroads tussle when Goliath tried to throttle him. He had such a placid nature, and was so patient and tolerant, shrugging his shoulders at adversity, that he should never have been mixed up in this tough fighting business.

I was angry, bitter and dejected and seeing Ginger and his mate Jock looking at the blood-covered mortar as though it had some contagious disease I snapped.

'Clean it off – both of you,' and then I added, as an afterthought: 'And sing "Bonnie Scotland" while you're at it.' It was a cruel jibe, but I was past feeling sensitive.

Lieutenant Bernard returned from company HQ, only about twenty yards behind, and urged us on.

'Time to move. Everybody up. Come on – on your feet. Spread out more.' Our tanks had finished shelling and machine-gunning the trees and the follow-up troops were static in the open, a juicy target for enemy 'stonks'. As we slowly advanced the ground rose quite sharply, and the extra effort made me sweat until my vest clung to my back and chest. Sporadic firing greeted our sections to the left and right, but we in the centre were remarkably lucky to meet no immediate opposition.

All around us the dense woodland was gloomy and dank, emitting an earthy tang suggestive of decaying vegetation that contrasted sharply with the acrid fumes of war. Our stupendous artillery bombardment had pulverized thousands of tree branches, many of which had crashed to the forest floor, impeding our progress. Other severed tree tops were poised perilously above our heads, ready to topple, while some had become interlocked to form an arboreal canopy, shutting out the light and making the forest even darker.

Lieutenant Bernard waved us down for a breather and to try to get his bearings. The platoon was widely scattered and under these conditions it was difficult to keep any shape or order. Our officer told us he was awaiting a recce report from a scout up ahead. While we waited I realized I was carrying the extra Bren and passed it over to Ginger's mate Jock.

'Sling your rifle over your shoulder and take this Bren,' I told him. 'You'll be glad of it if we hit trouble.' The spare mortar Ginger and I had retrieved was conveniently forgotten and no doubt someone following us would find it useful.

Our scout returned to say that the enemy was lying in wait on the crest of the rise we were climbing.

'Move out,' ordered the lieutenant, whereupon we edged forward cautiously, to be greeted first by small arms fire and then by Spandau bursts. The platoon began returning the fire and though we had somehow become bunched it was heartening to see so many buddies standing almost shoulder to shoulder hammering away. A sort of 'experienced professionalism' seemed to take over and I was thrilled and pleased to see everyone joining in.

'Keep going, keep going,' urged our platoon commander, waving one arm while firing his revolver with the other. We did keep going. What else could we do? In these circumstances a madness takes over, driving you on. Fear is no longer a foe, being somehow pushed into the background, to re-emerge only after the action is over.

The woodland thinned a little and at the top of the rise I could see a wounded German sitting against a tree, his face etched with pain and his arms raised limply in surrender. A German Red Cross man now appeared, running towards us. I heard a roar and saw Ginger, standing alongside me, staring wildly ahead and raising his rifle.

'No, no, Ginge,' I screamed, 'he's Red Cross.' The German ran to his wounded comrade and planted a large Red Cross flag in the ground nearby before dressing his wound.

Another original Bucks man, Jimmy Langford, from Yorkshire, was lying wounded. He looked pale, but was quite philosophical about it.

'Can you wait for the medics, Jim?' I called.

'Yeah Whitey, carry on. It's just me leg.' I felt a tinge of envy as I left him. He was out of it.

Lieutenant Bernard now dashed madly among us, as though possessed of a demon, waving his revolver and spurring us on.

'Last few yards chaps. Let's go to it. Run, run, as fast as you can,' he bawled. I glanced at Jock, to whom I had given the spare Bren. To my consternation he was carrying the gun by its handle, down by his side. It would be priceless now, at this crucial juncture, if we met any last-minute German heroes, or rather fanatics, prepared to die for Fuehrer and Fatherland. Not only was he taking no part in the attack, but he was not even ready to defend himself. I was furious.

'Get that bloody Bren up, you prat,' I screamed. He looked blankly towards me and pointed the gun forward. A few more spasms of fire and we had reached the crest of the rise and were descending the other side.

'Hold it here, spread out, watch your front,' senior NCOs called out. 'This is it for now. Dig in.'

I was still angry at Jock for failing to support us with the Bren and stormed over to him.

'You bastard!' I shouted. 'How dare you behave like that!' A red rage came over me, no doubt accelerated by all I had just been through, and I threw a punch, aimed at his chin. But my equipment restricted my movements and he half parried the blow. In stepping back he stumbled and fell over the branches around his feet. He merely picked himself up and scowled at me. I knew I was wrong to strike him; I could only attribute my unseemly behaviour to the shredded state of my nerves after seeing poor Ken and Larry lying horribly mutilated back there and the added purgatory of wading through the forest maelstrom.

Digging in was easy in the soft rich soil and soon we had deep, comfortable T-shaped 'slitters' – all, that is, except our newcomers, Ginger and Jock, whose clumsy, half-hearted efforts at digging-in made me cringe as I viewed their disordered, unfinished trench. God knows where they had been taught their infantry drill. Trying to make amends for my earlier callous behaviour I approached them.

'Look you two,' I said, 'me and Beachy will finish this off. You collect branches for the rest of us to cover our doovers.' They thought this a good idea and did as I suggested, so that soon the whole section had head cover in case the enemy sent over their wicked air bursts.

As darkness approached we gave some thought to food and look-outs and then our sergeant-major arrived.

'Rum ration, Whitey,' he whispered. Beachy, my old dig in buddy and I had a generous helping and then I distributed the remainder among the section. I left Ginger and Jock to the last and was surprised to find their doover empty and the Bren lying on its side in the soil. Had they done a 'runner', I wondered, or had the enemy taken them? German patrols in the past had proved adept at silently breeching our lines in the dark and making off with prisoners, so I did not lightly dismiss this theory. I visited the other sections, but no one had seen our two young lads and I therefore reported them as missing.

The Black Watch usually sent out a search party immediately anyone was thought to have gone 'on the trot'. By retracing the route in a Jeep or truck the military police usually caught up with the offenders. I never did find out what happened to Ginger and Jock. I was not overly concerned about their commitment and usefulness to the unit – or rather their lack of it – but I was angry that the majority of our reinforcements lacked guts and 'moral fibre', as the experts called it. After all, the war was half over. We old hands had done the lion's share of the fighting.

Dawn slowly nudged away the night and I awoke, intensely cold, to find a hoary frost covering the nearby shrubbery and a blanket I had draped over my shoulders the previous evening. Lieutenant Bernard called us together to explain the mystery of the missing 23-foot ditch that had puzzled us and our supporting tank in the early stages of the attack. The officer produced a poor quality map of the area and by the marked ditch it read 'ditch 2–3 feet wide' (two-to-three feet wide), but a dotted line had overprinted the hyphen between the two numbers, making it appear as though the figure was 23. As someone later remarked: 'Any silly bloody fool could make a mistake like that.'

While we were relaxing in or near our 'slitters', chatting idly and calling out to one another, several shells landed in the area, and then a single rifle shot rang out, causing Lieutenant Bernard to jump into the nearest trench.

'Jesus, that was bloody close,' he gasped. So it appeared that we were still under observation, but then word came through that the Germans, diabolically inventive as ever, had left microphones hidden in the trees to pick up our voices, enabling them to range their artillery accordingly. I had personal experience of this later when our sergeant asked me to go on a patrol with Beachy and young Jerrams to see if the track ahead was mined.

'How are we supposed to do that Sarge?' I asked.

'Use your prodders,' he answered.

'That's gonna take ages,' protested Beachy, 'and there's snipers about.'

'Why don't we spray the track with our Stens?' suggested young Jerrams, a bright and eager lad. 'We're bound to set off any Schu mines.'

'OK, do that,' said the sergeant. Not at all happy with the assignment, which we felt had been ill-conceived, we nevertheless crept forward. Soon we heard voices up the track and ducked behind a clump of shrubs. A German appeared, but behind him came two squaddies, loaded with map cases.

'Hi there,' we called and bounded out from the bushes on to the track. The two squaddies were surprised and relieved to see us, but then, almost immediately, we heard 'Woop-woop', the noise a mortar bomb makes as it turns at the top of its trajectory before falling to earth. We all flattened as two bombs exploded near the patch we had just left.

'Keep your voices low,' said one of the squaddies, a corporal.

'It's the "mechanical men". Jerry has put them all over the area.'
He was referring to the microphones our platoon had
experienced earlier. The two squaddies were from a recce unit
and the German had surrendered to them while they were
wandering about trying to get their bearings. It was their
prisoner who had sportingly warned them about the 'mechanical
men'. We thanked the squaddies for doing our job; by walking
along the track they had proved it was free from mines. Our
platoon HQ warmly welcomed them on their return with us,
since their knowledge of this jungle-like area with its
'mechanical men' could prove invaluable.

After a big push, like the one in which we had just
participated, we usually had several days' respite before going
back in the line, but now there seemed to be a general state of
turmoil. Our sergeant, looking worried, came over to Shorty and
me.

'Get your men kitted up with ammo. We're moving off soon.'

'What's up Sarge?' asked Shorty.

'Some talk about the Gordons refusing to go in,' he said. 'So
we're taking their "push", but it's all confusing.' We were
flabbergasted; everyone was feeling the strain of keeping
pressure on the enemy, but refusing to continue was
unbelievable. Surely there must be a reason. And there was.

As we pushed through the Gordons' positions, along a track
busy now with vehicles, we saw a four-foot high pile of bodies,
neatly stacked, head to toe, and still being built. There must
have been thirty or forty corpses in the pile.

'That's how I like to see the Jerries – piled high,' said Beachy
to the Gordons, who were standing about, looking sullen.

'Trouble is,' said one of them, 'they're our lads.' We later
heard the full story. A line of about twenty Germans with hands
raised had walked towards the Jocks to surrender. Our lads
rushed forward, slinging their weapons over their shoulders to
free both hands for ransacking the prisoners. At the last moment
the Germans flung themselves to the ground and other
Germans, fully armed with automatics, emerged from cover and
mowed down the Jocks. Even squaddies further back, not
directly involved, were caught unawares and sent reeling.

Some squaddies were consumed by the desire to loot
prisoners, stopping at the height of a battle to take watches,
rings, money and other valuables. But this time they had been

made to pay dearly for their booty. It was not an outright refusal by the Gordons to go on. They were too badly shaken by the mini-massacre and in any case were now well below strength. Apart from the dead we saw, other Jocks must have been wounded, drastically reducing their numbers.

Just past the Gordons we rested briefly before tackling the final 250 yards of forest. Squaddies wandered into the thick undergrowth to answer nature's call, but I went among the trees for another reason. I thought of Ken Ware and Larry Crowther and all my other mates tragically lost on the long haul from Normandy's beaches. In that lonely retreat I became completely overwhelmed by it all and broke down, sobbing bitterly. But there were no tears, which might at least have helped me shake off these feelings of abject despair, triggered no doubt by the sight of the Gordons' heaped bodies. How much more could my demented mind withstand?

Back in the line NCOs were summoned and put in the picture. A creeping barrage would be laid down to help us take the final stretch of forest, after which we would be facing open fields and scattered farms. To cap it all our company was to be point company, with my section in the lead. I looked around at my friends; it was evident from their grim faces that they too viewed with alarm the prospect of our unit leading across those open fields.

The artillery officer arranging the creeping barrage was chasing around with Lieutenant Bernard, organizing us among the trees into an arrowhead formation, with my section out front and me the tip of the arrow.

'The barrage will start any minute now,' shouted the gunnery officer. 'Move off when I tell you.' He spoke into a field telephone while we waited, each man behind a tree. Suddenly, with a mighty crash, the shells started landing among us, showering us with soil and twigs.

'Christ! What's happening?' someone yelled.

'Bugger this, they're dropping short. Let's get out of it,' another voice cried. In unison the section turned and ran, doubled up, about twenty yards back, where our company commander stood with the artillery officer.

'What's going on?' demanded the officers.

'The fucking things fell among us. What are you fucking playing at you bastards?' In those few seconds we blasted off at the officers, not caring what we said. Had Field Marshal Montgomery himself been present we would have treated him with the same disrespect. Incredibly we had sustained no casualties from the misdirected shell fire.

'It's all right now,' soothed the artillery officer in a quieter tone, 'they'll be moving forward.' He talked into his phone to adjust the fall of shot. But our company commander was not so sympathetic or understanding.

'Get back to your positions,' he ordered angrily, drawing his revolver and waving it in a threatening manner. Reluctantly we returned to our original positions and once the barrage reopened – this time well ahead of us – we negotiated the rest of the Reichswald Forest without opposition.

We paused at the edge of the trees, weighing up a farmhouse in a field, about fifty yards ahead. A second lone farmstead was situated another hundred yards further on, a little to the left. Stepping out from the cover of the trees, we advanced in line towards the first building. Once in the open I braced myself for the inevitable Spandau fire, and it did not fail me, though it was obviously not coming from our immediate objective. The machine-gun's chilling, unmistakable sound – almost like cloth being ripped – always sent a shiver through me, even when it was not firing in my general direction. The legendary Spandau, or MG42 to give the gun its official designation, fired at the amazing rate of 1,200 rounds per minute (compared with our Bren's 500–600), and was yet another excellent German weapon.

On this particular occasion, as the platoon edged towards the farmhouse, spread out in line, the machine-gun's long burst caught several lads further up the line and I heard them cry out as they fell. The rest of us promptly bunched up behind the farm building, where we were pinned down as the bullets ricocheted off walls, zipped through windows and kicked up the soil on either side.

Lieutenant Bernard disappeared into the farmhouse and came out with two Germans, who looked petrified. Several of our lads punched them in anger and the prisoners, with their hands held high, ran round to the front of the building and then hared off towards their own lines. It all happened so quickly we were caught napping. Though shots were fired at them, and one appeared to stumble, they made good their escape. Our officer was enraged and turned on Shorty and me.

'You and you, get your men and take that other farmhouse.' He pointed to the building across the fields where the Spandau seemed to be located. I was horrified at the thought of dashing across that open stretch, but there was no way out.

'OK 7 Section, follow me,' I shouted, and ran pell-mell across the field. When I was half-way across, a screaming German came out of the building holding up a badly shattered arm, and I spied an enemy armoured vehicle making a getaway at the rear. Ignoring the wounded German I shouted:

'Come on 7, don't bother with him.' I was only yards from our objective, filled with apprehension, when I turned round to urge my lads on, but was shocked to find I was alone; no one had supported me. On reaching the farm I found it empty and assumed that the Spandau fire had come from the armoured car. I beckoned to my section, still at the first farm.

'Come on, it's all clear,' I shouted. Johnny Reed, from Basingstoke, the company runner who later became a good pal, was the first to reach me.

'The company commander wants to know your name Corporal,' he gasped, breathless after his dash. I told him and thought no more about it. Some weeks later, I learned that I had been Mentioned in Dispatches 'for daring action in the face of the enemy'.

At last we were out of the Reichswald Forest. I was not aware at the time that our unit, the 1st Battalion Black Watch, had the distinction of being the first British unit on German soil, a feat which earned us a letter of congratulations from our Corps Commander, General Horrocks. We had also overcome the much-vaunted Siegfried Line, on which every squaddie had promised to hang out his washing in the popular song of the day.

10   Across the River Niers

After overcoming the tangled Reichswald Forest our platoon settled down for the night around an isolated farmhouse, with 8 Section stuck out in front and our section (7) and 9 on either side. We treated the building warily at first, for fear of boobies, but gradually we grew bolder and eventually used it for cooking with our little Tommy-cookers – any excuse to get out of those cursed holes in the ground. Each time we had dug in lately I wondered morbidly whether I was digging my own grave.

Spasmodic clusters of shells continued to harass us, which made me think that perhaps those confounded 'mechanical men' were still operating. S Platoon just behind us received extremely heavy shelling during the night, after which we heard the agonizing cries of one man, who sounded bewildered, pained and breathless. He repeatedly pleaded for help with such sobbing emotion that we called to each other from our doovers, debating whether to help him. But alarmed voices rang out:

'It's the stretcher-bearers' job' ... 'You'll never find him in the dark' ... 'How about if we get stonked out there? Who'll come for us?' It was fear, stark fear screaming out again and illustrating its amazing potency. Another salvo crashed down behind us, silencing altogether that faint, imploring voice. Fear had called the tune once more and it was lucky for us that we had listened.

During the dawn stand-to the tranquillity was rudely shattered by firing from the other side of the farmhouse, 9 Section's station, accompanied by screams and yells in English and German.

'Christ, what's happening?' asked Beachy, as we ducked low in our doover, thinking our turn was next. The battle subsided but then 8 Section's Bren, sited to our front, came to life and through the light mist I saw three figures stagger and fall. Other ghostly silhouettes raced on into no man's land. Apparently an enemy section had been hiding in the forest behind us – probably in a well-camouflaged dugout we had missed – and at dawn had made a dash for their own lines, coming up behind 9 Section. According to the section's only survivor our lads were caught completely off guard. Five Black Watch mates were killed and one wounded. The most bitter blow for me was the loss of another D-Day 'original', as we called ourselves. Fred Cousins, a salt-of-the-earth Devonian, and an inspiring corporal in charge of the section, was riddled from behind, his face still retaining the startled look brought on by the speed and abruptness of it all. We laid our mates under the farmhouse wall, covered with their groundsheets. Three Germans killed in the action were placed alongside them. In death there was no distinction.

We were shelled intermittently throughout the day and could only cower down and sweat it out. But I applied a basic infantry rule during heavy bombardments that the newer lads failed to follow: keep a sharp look-out for an enemy attack behind a barrage. God knows, we ourselves had often gone into action with a creeping barrage, which had proved effective. I therefore popped my head over the edge of our 'slitter' occasionally in 8 Section's direction, just ahead, and was perplexed to see arms stuck in the air from two of the four 'slitters'. I nudged Beachy.

'What's going on out there?' I asked.

'Can't you guess? I've seen blokes do it before.'

'Do what?' I asked naively.

'They're hoping to catch a Blighty wound. A bit of shrapnel in the arm or hand and it's home sweet home.' This was a foolproof way of attempting a self-inflicted wound and I decided to bear it in mind. The cracks in my morale were widening and I would go to almost any lengths to be out of this terrible madhouse.

In front of us lay the River Niers, about forty to fifty yards wide here, which we were to cross in Buffaloes (amphibious vehicles) during the night after our artillery had softened up the far bank. What a pasting our gunners gave the Germans! At about 1600 hours the bombardment started, continuing for several hours until the far bank was aflame. I felt thankful we never had to face the horrendous shelling the Germans received from our boys, whose sterling work made our job so much easier. As the campaign progressed through north-west Europe our bombardments seemed to increase in ferocity.

We moved down to the river-bank after dark and boarded the Buffaloes. I was always anxious about being on water with a full pack, since the prospects of survival would be slim if we sank, but my fears were groundless and apart from a few shells that created water spouts nearby the journey was uneventful. Now that we were on the Fatherland's sacred soil I expected the enemy to yield every inch of ground grudgingly, so it came as a tremendous surprise and bolstered morale when we saw about thirty Germans on the far bank with hands in the air, eager to board our Buffaloes for the return journey when we alighted.

But reality soon returned. As the platoon moved forward down a road we were fired on from behind and Lieutenant Bernard and our company commander were among the casualties. Fortunately our platoon commander was only nicked in the leg, but he had to go back for attention. The major, hit embarrassingly in the behind, continued to charge about like a mad bull, bellowing and insisting we eliminate the strongpoint before he would let the medics treat him. The firing was coming from the narrow window of a building we had just passed near a mill.

'Get the Piat over here,' yelled the major. He was lying in a hollow and flames from several fires lit up the scene vividly, showing his distorted face and the mill in the background.

'The Piat man's been hit sir,' said the sergeant.

'Well just bring me the bloody Piat,' ordered the company commander, whose wound was obviously making him extremely irritable. Some time earlier I had gladly relinquished my job as Piat man and did not volunteer to help out now, but as the sergeant passed, struggling with the Piat and a pack of bombs, he spotted me.

'Oh it's you Whitey,' he said with relief. 'You know the Piat. Grab this and get up to the major right away.' Cursing my bad luck I had no option but to take the Piat and crawl behind him.

'It's OK sir, Whitehouse knows the Piat,' said the sergeant on reaching the major.

'Right, put a bugger through that little window,' said the major pointing out the enemy's strongpoint. The sergeant primed and slid the bomb into place and I took aim and fired. It was a very narrow ground-floor window that reminded me of a castle's mullion window, but the bomb found its mark and exploded on the sill.

'Good lad,' said the company commander ecstatically, for the moment forgetting his wound. 'That's fixed the bastards.' The major seemed on a high and wanted to continue, but his backside was now soaked with blood and the stretcher-bearers, helped by the sergeant, finally managed to get him to lie face down on the stretcher and, still shouting orders, he was carried to the nearby mill, now being used by our MO and the German MO to tend the wounded of both sides.

We dug in and passed a fitful night, with sporadic shelling disturbing our sleep. After dawn's stand-to I was intrigued by the German machine-gunner who had remained at his post at the mullion window, when it seemed that all his comrades had fled. I found the spot from where I had fired the Piat and gazed across to the narrow slit. Then I walked over for a closer look and noted the chunk of masonry missing from the sill where the bomb had struck. I peered inside and was astonished by what I saw. There were three figures and a table and chair in the room forming a tableau. The Spandau was on the table, pointing towards the window and a German paratrooper sat on the chair, arms still in the firing position, one foot roughly bandaged and bloodsoaked, and his face staring blankly ahead. Two companions sat against the wall behind him and all three looked so alive I would not have been surprised had they spoken to me. I was almost tempted to say: 'OK chaps, you can come out now.' Once again it illustrated the devastating blast of the Piat bomb. Three brave men, I thought, but why had they stayed when so many of their comrades had either surrendered or fled?

As I turned away I spotted a fine-looking automatic rifle on the ground. Picking it up to admire it, I noticed it was in immaculate condition, with the bolt area still greased. Then, inexplicably, a kind of strange nausea swept over me. Why was I admiring this weapon, whose sole purpose was to kill people? I was sick of killing people. Barely able to stop myself from vomiting, I smashed the gun against the wall several times and threw it into the nearby undergrowth. I had often heard the expression 'a wave of nausea swept over him'. Now I knew exactly what it meant.

While we were eating our midday rations a clump of greenery

in the midst of our positions suddenly sprouted a pair of arms and a German paratrooper stood up from his one-man foxhole and surrendered. Remarkably, we had been walking within a few feet of him all morning, but he was well camouflaged – like a walking bush. I think the smell – and the sound – of our sizzling sausages must have brought him out of hiding.

Up ahead were several clumps of woods which we all hoped would be cleared by someone else, but it was not to be. We were ordered to make a sweep in that area during the night and the prospect filled me with trepidation. Wood clearing during the day is unpleasant; at night it is terrifying.

Luckily we cleared the woods without a hitch, though it was a miracle we never shot each other as we groped in the dark, flinching at ghostly shadows and the sharp snap of twigs underfoot. Moving from one wood to another we came across a huge ditch in a field and holed up there for the night. The ditch, which I could only assume to be an anti-tank ditch, was about ten feet wide and five feet deep and seemed ideal to me, but Shorty preferred our normal two-man 'slitters' and told his men to dig in about ten yards behind us. Later a company runner arrived with the order for us to stay in our present positions.

After an unsettled night I was able to take stock at daylight and looking round our field, surrounded by clumps of trees, I felt uneasy about our exposed position. To compound our problems we had no officer, Dutchy Holland, now a sergeant, and Shorty and me, the junior NCOs, being in charge of about twenty-five men. We had no idea where the rest of the company were and knew only the approximate location of company HQ, and hoped we would not have to make any crucial decisions.

Tommy-cookers were lit at the bottom of the wide ditch and porridge blocks plopped into boiling water while we awaited clarification from HQ, but no one came. Spandaus opened up as the morning mist dissipated and we could see enemy troops hiding behind trees just to our right and firing at squaddies, evidently from another platoon, in a separate clump of woods to our left. Unfortunately our lads were about 300 yards away – too far for us to be able to help, and my section and Shorty's could only watch as the firefight ahead of us hotted up, though one or two in my section did manage an occasional pot-shot at the fleeting field-grey figures. After a fierce exchange of fire between these two groups, a squaddie called out urgently, painfully to the enemy. Others joined in and one squaddie stood up, waving an arm limply. He was obviously wounded and wished to surrender. The Spandau fired again and he sank out of sight. Grey figures moved towards the woods, we heard grenade explosions and the shouting and shooting ceased. The Germans, bent double, retraced their steps and we noted that they were taking no Black Watch prisoners that day. Our two sections, stung into life, began sniping angrily at them.

'I haven't got much ammo, Whitey,' called one of my section. 'Nor me,' came the cry from several others. After a brief discussion among the NCOs, Beachy volunteered to dash back for supplies, hoping to locate company HQ in the area of the mill. About twenty yards from the left end of our ditch was a hayrick and Beachy thought that if he ran behind it and sprinted to the roadside ditch, he could gain access to the woods and safety.

'OK Beachy, go man go,' we shouted, urging him on. He was quickly up and over the edge of the ditch and in a mad gallop reached the hayrick, flopping down behind it. He looked back at us and gave a thumbs up sign, grinning broadly. But his expression changed to one of horror as enemy tracer bullets struck the rick, setting it alight. The only consolation was that the smoke from the crackling rick hid Beachy as he rushed back to us and flung himself in the ditch, breathless and lucky to make it.

'I can see their helmets shining,' cried our Bren gunner, young Eddie Head, a ruthless, chain-smoking Southampton lad. He began firing single shots at the coal-scuttle helmets, glinting in the early morning sun. Sergeant Dutchy Holland set up the two-inch mortar at the bottom of the ditch and put a bomb down the barrel. Then he quickly lifted the mortar on to the edge of the ditch, turned the firing knob and the bomb flew towards the woods. But the kick-back demolished the parapet edge and the mortar crashed down on Dutchy's knee. He gave a loud yelp and collapsed, but we were all too busy to help him.

I heard shouts and catcalling from Shorty's section behind us and looking round saw a sight to gladden the heart. Our mates from 8 Section had put their tin hats on the end of their mine prodders and were slowly waving them from side to side, almost like a fairground coconut shy.

Every time I peered over the lip of the trench, Sten at the

ready, I felt shots zip past my head, and was unable to reply. Beachy and Gerry Cole, on each side of me, were also having difficulty getting their heads up to fire.

'Some bugger's got this spot weighed up,' muttered Coley. He was a likeable Lancashire lad who had become a father two weeks earlier. We three were in the middle of the long trench, receiving so much enemy attention that I began to wonder whether some smart German assumed that this sector must be the command spot.

'Let the three of us pop up quick, fire a short burst and duck,' suggested Beachy.

'Right,' I said. 'One, two, three, up!' It was a marvellous way of relieving the frustration, but as we ducked down we heard a strange sizzling sound and a silvery cylinder, about six inches long and resembling a cigar tube, plopped in to the trench at our feet. Nobody moves quicker than a squaddie in such circumstances. We dived frantically in all directions, but nothing happened. Gingerly creeping back to peer at the strange object, we came to the conclusion that it was a type of rifle grenade that had failed to explode.

I moved to the far right of the ditch, where Eddie Head was still excited about the glistening helmets and the Piat pair were busy blasting their bombs in the far woods. This end of the ditch was receiving no retaliatory fire and I thought perhaps the Germans, having seen Beachy attempt to leave from the other end, were concentrating their fire in that direction.

Other lads were now joining in the shiny-hat-shooting. Evidently, as the enemy had come through the dew-laden woods their helmets had become wet, giving them a lustre in the morning light. The Germans' carelessness was surprising; they were normally so proficient at camouflage.

'I'm down to one mag, Corp,' someone shouted.

'You're lucky, I'm out altogether,' came another voice.

'No Piat bombs, Whitey.' I looked at Sergeant Holland, in obvious pain with his injured knee. The firing from the woods had stopped. Had we won? Was there any need to panic about the ammunition shortage?

'Look out, here they come. Enemy front,' yelled Gerry Cole. My heart sank when I saw the figures dashing towards us from the far trees. As we stood transfixed Eddie Head snapped us out of our inertia.

'I'm not fucking dying in here,' he shouted, clambering out of the ditch and levelling his Bren from the hip. Most of us followed his example, and those still with ammunition fired off a few rounds. We ran several yards towards the advancing foe – God knows why – shouting and cursing deliriously to give vent to our anger and frustration. Then above the din I heard a shout:

'Stop firing, they're our blokes.' We had braced ourselves to do battle with the raiders, but these were squaddies. As they approached I recognized one lad, but he held a bloody field dressing to his jaw and lower lip and was unable to speak. Several others were wounded, though none seriously, and some were in shirt sleeves, suggesting they had left in a hurry.

'The bastards came behind us,' one of them explained. 'They must have crept in through the night.' The alarming thing was that we never knew this platoon of ours was in the woods up ahead. Two of their number, Corporals Lock and Lockie, giants towering well over six feet each, had stayed behind. They were wild characters, noted for their recklessness, and would no doubt give a good account of themselves.

We settled back into our anti-tank ditch, leaving the other platoon, or rather its remnants, to return to HQ with a message to send ammunition to us urgently. With time now to think I was angry at the lack of contact with our officers or anyone from HQ, less than half-a-mile away. Surely it was up to them to send someone to check the situation.

While we waited I realized I had German binoculars and a Luger in my blouse inner pockets and thought it wise to bury them in case we were overrun. I was not averse to 'confiscating' such items – and knives – from prisoners, but I drew the line at watches, jewellery and similar personal possessions. Other lads followed my example, realizing that the enemy would give us a rough ride if they found us with looted gear. Then, out of the blue, we heard an unmistakable clanking noise across the fields.

'Bloody hell, tanks,' said Beachy. The very word always had me petrified. With any amount of ammunition and all the will in the world we would be powerless against the dreaded Panzers. I looked at Dutchy and Shorty, who had now joined us. Three NCOs had to make a snap decision.

'No use staying,' I said. Shorty nodded agreement.

'OK, let's get back to the other woods,' ordered Dutchy. 'And bring all the weapons.' Someone helped the injured sergeant out of the ditch and supported him as we trekked back the few hundred yards to the woods we had cleared the previous night. A few light shells and mortars kicked up dirt around us, but once in the woods we felt safe. Shorty accompanied Dutchy to HQ to assess the situation, and get treatment for the sergeant's injured knee, while the rest of us, including the remnants of the platoon chased out earlier, sat around two dugouts previously occupied by the Germans. They were well-made, T-shaped trenches, covered at one end with logs and soil.

A red-tabbed staff officer with red hatband, Sam Browne belt and cane strolled towards us. He was tall, very severe-looking and, surprisingly, alone. As he drew near we stood up and I saluted him. He looked around and seeing that I was the only NCO present he spoke to me.

'What happened then corporal? Why did you come out?'

'There were tanks messing about up there sir,' I replied. 'We've knocked some of their infantry back, but we've no ammo left, and there's no officer. Just me and two other NCOs.'

'Right, we'll get you fixed up, but you'll have to retake those positions tonight.' And so saying the officer turned on his heel and left us. I realized he had no inkling of our recent harrowing ordeal, nor did he express any feelings or offer us encouragement.

Reaction began to set in after the morning's trials. A depression settled over us, affecting men in different ways. I was generally feeling out of sorts, ill-tempered and grouchy. With some the shakes started in the legs and talking came through chattering teeth. Others spoke rapidly, as if to show that they were unaffected, when in reality their actions gave them away. A few became introspective and sullen, saying very little, while several disappeared into the trees to be alone. Gerry Cole was jittery and talked about his new son.

'Why don't we have a little prayer meeting, Stan?' he suggested. 'It will do us good and certainly can't do any harm.' I felt embarrassed, since my faith was now non-existent. I had entered the army as a 16-year-old Sunday school teacher – not a fanatic, but certainly a genuine believer. Now I had forsaken religion, reasoning that any God who could allow so much agony, so much death and misery throughout the world was not worth knowing.

'Please yourself Gerry,' I said, 'but count me out.' He asked around and surprisingly nearly a dozen lads agreed to his suggestion. They gathered together and each offered up a little prayer, Gerry asking that his new-born son be preserved and that he might see the boy soon. I was walking away from the group when a spine-chilling sound wailed across the countryside. The Moaning Minnies were after us. Of all war-like noises perhaps the scream of the multi-barrelled *Nebelwerfers* was the most terrifying and turned my blood to water. I had heard these mortars many times before, but was unable to master my fear of them. I could face ordinary shelling quite well, but these devils had me quivering from head to toe. I looked up towards the noise and thought I saw two black objects lazily homing in on us.

With the speed of light the prayer meeting lads hurtled into the ex-German dugout nearest to them. Having strolled a few yards during the prayers I was furthest away and was about to follow them when I saw that the dugout was full. With those wailing screams tearing through my head I turned to the other dugout, about ten yards away. My feet bore wings for half the distance and as I neared the dugout an almighty bang shook the ground, the blast flinging me into the doover on top of several others. Stones and lumps of turf followed me in.

'Bloody hell, that was close,' said someone. I felt reassured on seeing my two closest pals, Shorty and Beachy, the former having rejoined us after leaving Dutchy at the RAP. What would I do without these two around me, I wondered? We seemed to give each other added strength, and if anything happened to either of them I knew it would be the end for me. I would just walk away from this bloody way of living – and dying – and bugger the consequences. We each exchanged a grim little look, straight in the eyes, as usual drawing extra encouragement from the barely perceptible nod and tight smile that followed. While further thudding explosions followed, we cowered in the well-constructed doover, thankful that the Germans were past masters at making secure dugouts. We sat huddled together in silence, brushing soil and turf from our clothes.

'Listen, what's that?' asked Beachy. A voice so faint and weak that it was barely audible reached us.

'Help, help,' I could just make out, though it sounded some way off.

'That's Jerry calling from the edge of the wood,' said Shorty. 'Crafty bugger. It's a trick.'

'Help, somebody help.' There it was again, so faint and distant. Being nearest the doover opening I poked my head out towards the sound. I could see shattered tree branches lying about and a steel helmet between us and the other dugout, but everything seemed quiet.

'Nothing happening here,' I murmured to the others while looking further afield towards where we assumed the Germans were calling. The others joined me and the feeble calls came again, now breathless and desperate.

'Christ, it's coming from the other dugout,' I shouted, scrambling out on all fours. I crawled along the ground until I reached a shallow crater on the edge of the dugout. It was almost a direct hit.

Ever since Ginger Thompson had rolled on top of me, shattered by a mortar bomb in the Scottish Highlands, I had experienced monumental shocks. And coming through France, Belgium and Holland I had met some unexpected, gruesome sights, but nothing prepared me for the dreadful scene I now beheld. I felt a physical blow between my eyes and my head went back on my neck. The nearest bodies were so compacted that it was impossible to pull them apart, and the heads and necks were the same width. Right at the back, in the covered part of the dugout, was a blood-covered apparition, calling out faintly and trying to struggle over the bodies of his mates. I had to kneel on the others to stretch out for him, but his leg was protruding rigidly and the dugout had insufficient head room to allow him out.

'We need help here,' I said to the others, who had followed me over and looked equally stunned. 'I'll go to the RAP.' It was a good excuse for me to flee this carnage, and before anyone else could steal my reason for leaving I ran off towards the mill and the RAP.

At the mill, being used to tend the wounded, the MO was calling softly to a squaddie lying on his stomach on a stretcher, a six-inch piece of jagged shell splinter protruding from between his shoulder blades. There was no response. The MO looked at the two lads who had brought the wounded man in.

'He's gone lads. There's another six inches inside him,' he said quietly. 'You'd better get back to your company.' The two lads looked disbelievingly at the MO and then at each other. One bit his lip hard and lowered his head; the other, unable to control himself, sobbed:

'Oh Charlie, Charlie, the fucking bastards!' With heads drooping and struggling with their emotions they walked out. The MO turned to me.

'What's up with you?' he asked.

'Nothing for me,' I babbled. 'One of our dugouts has had a direct hit and we can't get the wounded from under the dead. We need stretcher-bearers.' My voice sounded strange, and I was prattling on in quick staccato phrases.

'And where is this dugout?' the MO asked.

'In the woods. Come on, I'll show you,' I rattled on.

'No, I can't come,' he said firmly, 'and all my teams are out.' He stared directly into my eyes and sighed.

'Would you like a cup of tea?' In retrospect I realize that shock must have dilated my eyes to the size of saucers. I could not believe my luck; the MO was asking me to wait and have a hot drink. No need to return just yet to that butcher's shop in the ground.

'Here you are laddie, drink this and take these tablets. They'll calm you down a little.' I would have taken arsenic right then had he offered it. In that soundproof basement, away from the bestiality and the torment, I was in another world, sitting on a sack of grain sipping hot tea. Looking into the mug I mused at the strange tricks fate can play. When the Moaning Minnies came over it was by sheer good luck that I had found the first dugout – the fateful one – too full. And how ironic that all the lads at the prayer meeting were now dead or severely wounded. Private Gerry Cole must have had a premonition, a not uncommon occurrence. How would his wife take the news? She had become a mother and a widow in the space of two weeks. Young Jerrams (Baby-face, we called him) had gone too, another smashing lad cut off before life had really begun. The only consolation was that it had been quick. I drained my mug as four stretcher-bearers struggled in with another casualty.

'Will two of you go with this chap? A messy job, I think,' said the MO.

'We know, we've seen it,' answered one. 'We've pulled two wounded out, but they're hysterical. I've had to sedate them. We'll bring them in now.' I walked back with the medics, but avoided the repulsive dugout, keeping my mind occupied by trying to reorganize our much-depleted section.

A new officer, Lieutenant Morgan, joined us in the evening, my first impression being that he was a likeable little fellow, though he must have been shocked and disquieted at our melancholy state. We recrossed the fields after dark, back to and beyond our anti-tank ditch positions and into the woods from where we had been fired on that morning. I was too dejected and battle-weary to care, going through the motions in mechanical fashion, almost like a robot.

We occupied former German dugouts and settled down for the night. Lieutenant Morgan called us over and while we were chatting he struck a match and lit a cigarette.

'Bloody hell sir, be careful,' I said. He looked at me rather disdainfully.

'He knows we're here Corporal.'

'Maybe sir, but not to the bloody inch.' He smiled and nodded and snuffed out the cigarette.

'You're right,' he said. It was obvious our new officer had a lot to learn. Many of the lads smoked, finding that a 'drag' helped soothe frayed nerves, though I had not acquired the habit, having tried it without receiving any beneficial effects earlier in the campaign. The old superstition still persisted of not lighting three cigarettes with one match, a superstition that apparently originated in the earlier 1914–18 war when German snipers were vigilant for smokers at night. By the time a third Tommy was lighting up the enemy marksman had his sights well and truly lined up.

At dawn I was pleased to see the Guards Armoured tanks fanning out in the open spaces between the clumps of woods. And our sister battalion, the Argylls, took over the lead, leaving us to gather our wits and meagre resources and 'count heads'. One of our lads wandered off to answer nature's call and ran back gasping that he had stumbled on the bodies of Corporals Lock and Lockie, captured earlier, it seems. They had been shot in the back, perhaps trying to escape.

Several of us decided to return to the anti-tank ditch to retrieve souvenirs we had hidden, including my binoculars and a Luger. On the way there Eddie Head, prowling about the edge of a wood, gave a shout.

'Come and see what I've found,' he called out. We rushed

over and saw four coal-scuttle helmets, each pierced by a bullet, with blood and hair on the inside. A further search revealed four similar helmets, but no bodies. Nevertheless, eight Germans, shot in the head by Eddie's Bren aiming at those shiny helmets, somehow evened the score after the Moaning Minnies' slaughter.

Our magnificent stretcher-bearer, Tom King (Sergeant Tom, we now called him), came out with his team to collect the bodies of Corporals Lock and Lockie. He paused at our positions and looking distraught told us of his grisly ordeal in helping the battalion Red Cross empty the dugout after the Moaning Minnies had done their worst.

'I've never seen anything like it,' he said, shaking his head. 'All the limbs were blasted out of their sockets. It was like trying to handle sacks of crimson jelly.'

It was Tom who told me of the difficult choice he sometimes had to make when several wounded men needed attention at the same time, and when minutes could be precious in saving lives. If one man was calling 'stretcher-bearer' and another crying out for his mother he invariably gave preference to the man asking for the stretcher-bearer. Experience told him that a soldier calling for his mother was usually severely wounded and probably dying anyway. It was strange how men of all nationalities, when badly hurt, cried out for their mother, never their father or their wife, always their mother. I had heard badly wounded Germans calling out '*Mutter, Mutter*', and it was often the last word they ever uttered.

We tried to regroup, lick our wounds and cry, but the tears refused to come – certainly in my case. Once more I had to push recent calamitous events down into the deepest recesses of my mind, little realizing that there would come a time when those events would have to surface – or I would go mad.

The battalion took a breather and we visited the divisional mobile baths, where, after a hot soaking and change of socks and underwear, I stood talking to a couple of recent replacements. One of them nudged his mate.

'Take a squint at this prat, Harry. They must be bloody desperate for sergeants.' I looked at the slight, insignificant figure approaching us rather sluggishly. To my surprise I saw it was Pikey, now a sergeant, whom I had first met during our initial training at Colchester Barracks, more than two years earlier. Drill sergeants gave up in despair trying to get those rounded shoulders – almost a small hump – into some semblance of military bearing. His army-issue wire-framed glasses sat on a ruddy, cherubic face that had made me want to put an arm round him and say:

'For Christ's sake, Pikey, why don't you ask for an office or storeman's job?' The two lads standing alongside me had obviously missed the Military Medal ribbon on the sergeant's left breast and I said nothing as he ambled towards us, his face as angelic as ever and his toes still turned in as he walked.

I recalled those hectic days at Colchester on the assault course as we all leapt off the ten-foot wall, leaving poor Pikey, with tears in his eyes, peering at the ground far below through his wire-framed glasses. Every day he had to endure the taunts and jeers of the other lads and we all felt that it was just a matter of time before he requested a transfer or went 'on the trot'. But we soon discovered that Pikey was brave, with a stubborn streak that would not let him quit.

One evening, as we all set out for town, spruced up to entice the local girls, we spotted Pikey on top of the high wall, rocking backwards and forwards, hands clenching and unclenching as he stared down at the sandpit. We paused for a moment to watch and one or two shouted encouragement while others scoffed. Finally Pikey sat on the wall, turned on his belly and dropped off.

'Bleedin' wanker!' someone muttered as we continued into town. The next evening Pikey was on the wall again, still trying unsuccessfully to conquer his fear of that ten-foot drop, and on the free Saturday morning he was perched on the wall once more. I had to admire his gritty determination.

'Come on, let's give the poor bugger a hand,' I said to my mate Jimmy Caswell. When we climbed up to Pikey we saw that he had tears in his eyes. But there was something else too: his jaw was set and he had a steely look that suggested he would not let this obstacle beat him. Jimmy and I stood one each side of him.

'Come on Pikey,' said Jimmy. 'Give us yer hand. Take his other hand Whitey. We'll just drop off.' By now the sweat was rolling down Pikey's face.

'One, two, three – go!' I called, and we dropped off the wall.

The little chap's face lit up like a bright full moon as we stood up.

'Let's go again,' he said eagerly. We repeated the exercise several times and eventually Pikey was away on his own, flinging himself off the wall with reckless abandon. And that is how it was with him; whatever the odds he refused to be beaten. He was a natural prey for bullies, but he would turn on them sternly.

'Look friend, I'd go away if I were you,' he would warn. It usually worked, since there was something about his expression, and his body language, that deterred bullies. But one day in the canteen two strapping young men took no heed of his warnings and Pikey backed into a corner and raised his tightly-clenched fists.

'OK, come on,' he said calmly. 'I suppose I'll last five minutes with you two, but believe me, it'll be five minutes you'll remember all your bloody lives.' He crouched forward slightly, looking even smaller than his 5 ft 5 in, his chin set and his lower lip pouted. The two squaddies glanced round at the rest of us, watching intently, and found the excuse they badly needed.

'He's got all his bloody mates here, Charlie,' said one. 'You wouldn't be so brave on your own,' he continued, glaring at Pikey. 'Come on Charlie, leave the little bugger with his cronies. We'll see him again.' To catcalls and gibes from those of us watching, the two bullies stormed out.

After our training Pikey and I went to different companies and we lost touch altogether when I joined the Black Watch and he chose the Seaforths, but the story of his winning the Military Medal filtered through. It happened in the Reichswald Forest, where by now he was a corporal. While on look-out with a new lad, twenty or thirty yards ahead of his section's 'slitters', the front was so quiet that Pikey decided to strip and clean the Bren. The pair were sheltering behind a huge fallen tree trunk upon which Pikey placed each part prior to polishing and oiling. Suddenly a slight rustling among the trees ahead alerted them.

'Bloody hell – Jerries!' whispered the private, looking aghast at the dismantled Bren.

'Shhh! Creep back quietly and warn the lads,' whispered the corporal. As the young soldier moved off he was spotted by the enemy and fired on, whereupon the action began. Pikey calmly reassembled the Bren, placed a mag in position and opened fire, wiping out the probing patrol.

Now Sergeant Pike MM was approaching me, head down, while the two lads standing alongside me refused to believe that such a puerile, inferior little runt could gain three stripes.

'Good morning Sergeant Pike,' I said, holding out my hand. 'Congratulations on your MM.' My two buddies were more shocked and bewildered than ever. Pikey looked at me closely for a few seconds, his eyes squinting through those wire frames.

'Oh it's you Whitey,' he said, finally recognizing me. He moved close in and we hugged each other. We chatted for a while, mostly about old buddies, who was left and who had gone, sparing each other any gory details.

'Smashin' to see you again, Whitey,' he called out as he went on his way, giving us a clear view of those rounded shoulders.

'Yeah, take care Pikey,' I called after him, feeling a lump come to my throat. Good old Pikey, I thought. Three stripes and the MM. What a bloke.

'Y'know him Whitey?' asked one of my mates.

'Yeah,' I said. 'I know Pikey well. Let's have a tea and wad and I'll tell you all about Sergeant Pike MM.'

11   A Spot of Leave

When we entered the German town of Goch one night it had already seen bitter house-to-house fighting involving our sister battalions. I was appalled at the devastation and the raging fires, caused by bombing and shelling – both ours and the enemy's. It was noticeable that enemy artillery barrages were becoming fiercer and as we skirted giant heaps of rubble and dodged burst water mains we had to fling ourselves to the ground at the constant scream of shells.

The German *Volkssturmer* – the equivalent of our Home Guard, comprising the very old and the very young – were also becoming prominent and making a nuisance of themselves, usually brandishing bazookas, and despite their extreme age they had to be dealt with severely. Several times distraught families berated us unmercifully when they came to collect the bodies of their menfolk before our tanks crushed them.

'You have killed an old man,' they protested tearfully, shaking their fists and glowering at us. We could only shrug and point to the bazooka lying beside the corpse. We had to be equally firm in dealing with mere schoolboys, brandishing weapons almost too big for them to handle.

The reflected glow of Monty's Moonlight, bouncing off low, scudding clouds, lit up the whole scene of desolation with a pale, sickly hue and our faces, tinged with a silvery-blue sheen, made us look like a ghostly army from the nether regions going about their nocturnal work.

Our objective, a row of gaunt houses, silhouetted in stark relief against the flickering skyline, loomed about thirty yards ahead. Lieutenant Bernard, our platoon commander, who had returned after being slightly wounded at the Niers mill, slithered over to a group of about a dozen of us crouched behind some rubble.

'This is bloody murder chaps, but we've got to take those houses,' he said. 'Sergeant Lane and Redman [Reddy to us] have already gone forward, so when you're right follow me.' He ran for shadowy ground beneath a gable end that Monty's Moonlight had somehow missed, and without any pretence at organization or conformity we followed. Bravely he led us into the end house, firing through the door as he went. Trying to emulate his shining example, we dashed from house to house, screaming and giving each other moral support by our oneness in this hair-raising business of street fighting. All the houses were empty except the last, where we found the bodies of Sergeant Lane and Reddy lying in the cellar, riddled by automatic fire.

Sergeant Lane had been a Regular with over twenty years' service, having joined as a boy. Sadly he had become an alcoholic, his weekly allowance of one or two bottles of whisky and whatever liquor he could loot along the way proving his downfall. Reddy was his close friend, a friendship that could only spring up between fellow alcoholics.

Apparently the pair had staggered towards the enemy houses with the sergeant's Sten hanging around his knees, both drunkenly shouting:

'Come out you bastards, come out!'

No doubt they had made straight for the cellar, which often yielded up the liquor they craved, and going down the steps they were obviously watched and followed. As one of our lads put it: 'They lived for the stuff and they died for the stuff.' When we later examined them more closely we noted that their faces bore idiotic grinning expressions as though they were pleased that the death-wish they had flaunted for so long had finally been granted.

In the garden of this last house we found the body of Little Vic Woodley, shot in the back, presumably by the killers of Sergeant Lane and Reddy. Little Vic, a Cockney and one of our 'white hanky' lads, earlier had a sad tale to tell us. Just before the war he opened a delicatessen, but it failed and he was called up – all 5 feet and 7½ stone of him. When he went home on leave he had lost his house key and sat in a nearby café to await his wife's return. She eventually reeled past the café window in a drunken state, with a Canadian soldier supporting each arm. Little Vic watched them stagger into his house, sat and thought for a brief moment, then gathered up his kit and returned to his unit. He started divorce proceedings and arranged matters so that in the event of his death the lady would receive no pension. Well, he was dead now, and I mused on all the fine young men I had known – almost thirty – who had been killed in action. Perhaps there was more than a grain of truth in the old adage that the good die young.

There was none of today's counselling for the shock and pain of seeing 'brothers' shot or blown to pieces; no counselling for the shredded nerves or the nightmares before the next attack. The day was arriving when the original 'family' of 6 Platoon would no longer exist. Maybe half a dozen pale-faced, weary men slouch together away from the bustle and chatter of the replacements – the reinforcements! Tired eyes assess the newcomers, who are weighed in the balance and usually found wanting. The veterans watch the new 'sergeant father' come along with his clipboard trying to reallocate men and sections. He moves over to the battle-weary group, their features hinting at a succession of horrors endured, their body language – or lack of it – confirming those expressions. Sitting still, subdued, they meet the sergeant's questioning look with their own jaded stares. One of them speaks softly:

'Just keep us together. OK Sarge?' It is more an order than a request. The NCO pauses and glances at them again, sensing an aura emanating from the group. Half a dozen pairs of eyes rest on his own and that strange sensation touches him again.

'No problem chaps,' he says, writing on his clipboard. He was unable to explain how he felt then, but spoke about it later to his officer.

'I felt as though I was in the presence of ghosts,' he confided. The officer nodded and tapped his pen on the map in front of him.

'You probably were,' he finally said.

After recovering the bodies of Sergeant Lane and Reddy from the cellar we laid them, along with Little Vic's, against the wall of the last house and covered them with their groundsheets. Reddy's dad later wrote asking our officer for his son's tam o' shanter, which unfortunately had been buried with him. To pacify a grieving father the lieutenant sent him the bonnet of a squaddie killed more recently, making sure first that it had no giveaway identification marks.

'Dig in – as fast as you can,' ordered Lieutenant Bernard as we stood in some gardens, but the incoming fire was so intense that we had difficulty staying on our feet to scratch a hole.

'Bugger this for a lark,' said Beachy, 'let's get back inside.' We all rushed to the houses we had just combed and found signallers, drivers of abandoned trucks and other personnel all with the same idea of sheltering from the murderous artillery fire. Our officer spotted me.

'Ah Whitey,' he said, 'the 53rd Welsh will be pushing through shortly and then it's us again I'm afraid. So get your section ammoed up, and let me know who's LOB' (left out of battle). He was looking haggard, I noticed, but something else struck me. I was seeing him as if through binoculars, not with any variation in distance, but surrounded by a strange greyness. I turned to others near me and they too were enclosed in a hazy film.

I went out into the garden to see if my impaired vision had been a trick of the gloomy conditions. But no; as I focused on two men standing a little way off they became blurred and I realized that this was tunnel vision. I approached the two squaddies, Jack Allison and Jock Logie, and they seemed to be threatening each other, their Stens in a menacing attitude.

'What the bloody hell's going on?' I asked. They looked at me with expressions of despair.

'It's no good, we can't take any more,' groaned Jack. 'We're gonna shoot each other's legs.'

'Oh for Christ's sake, you two, lay off,' I said. We heard marching feet and voices singing 'Guide Me Oh Thou Great Jehovah' coming down the road in front of the houses.

'Listen,' I said firmly, 'the Welsh lads are coming through. We'll get a break now, so bloody well forget it. Right?' Jack Allison walked away sobbing, and Logie turned to me, tight lipped.

'Ah'm no' goin' any further forward, Whitey. Please yersel' whether ye report me or no'. Ah'm away tonight.'

'I know how you feel Jock,' I said. 'I'm falling apart myself. I can't see properly and I'm off to find an MO. Are you coming?'

'Ay,' he replied. 'Let's go.' Our artillery was repaying the Germans with interest now as we scrambled and scurried back the half-mile or so to battalion HQ, in a partially demolished house. I went into the MO's quarters and explained my problem.

'Ah yes, I see. You're just over-tired and over-stressed,' said the doctor in a condescending tone. 'We all are. Take these two tablets and you'll soon be fine.' He handed me two tiny tablets and a tumbler of water, and that was it. As I drained the glass an orderly barged in.

'I knew it wasn't you sir,' he gasped.

'What wasn't me?' asked the MO, puzzled.

'Somebody's just driven off in your car sir.' The MO shot out of the room in a fury and I followed, intending to tell Jock that he would have to wait while the MO tried to recover his car. But Jock was nowhere in sight. Then I realized he had 'done a runner' – in style in the MO's car.

As I reluctantly returned to the platoon I felt happy for Jock and fervently hoped that he would make good his getaway. I would have needed little persuasion to join him in his madcap escapade. Meandering back, with heavy step and heavier heart, dodging heaps of rubble, I grew bitter and angry. Why could they not see when a man had given his all? Squaddies like Allison and Logie were ready to cripple each other rather than endure this harrowing front-line killing a minute longer. Others had brazenly held up their arms while under fire, hoping to catch a Blighty wound. Some had merely pointed a gun at their foot and blazed away, while poor Banger Brown and others like him had paid a heavier price for their actions.

My mate Beachy met me when I reached the garden adjoining platoon HQ.

'They want you on an O Group,' he said, 'and you're to say who's on LOB.'

'It's me and you Beachy,' I said determinedly. His face lit up.

'It'll be great if they accept us,' he said. 'I'm honestly thinking of doing the bunk. I'll go mad if I have much more of this.' Uncompromising fear was again rearing its ugly head as my pal stared at me with an anguished expression. I viewed him through my 'tunnels'.

'I'll tell you this mate,' I said, 'I've only had one LOB and I'm bloody well having this one – legally or otherwise.' Leaving selected men out of battle before a big push had begun soon after we landed in Normandy. I believe the practice originated in the Great War when key men were omitted from major battles so that in the event of severe casualties – not uncommon in that war – they could form the nucleus of a new unit.

More heavy shelling drove us back into the house our platoon had commandeered. It was crowded with battle-weary, bomb-happy squaddies and three German prisoners, one of whom, wounded in the foot, had been brought in by his two comrades while I was with the MO. In my confused mental state it seemed obvious to me that this man had deliberately shot himself and his companions had seized the chance of avoiding further action by supporting him as he came across to our lines. I was incensed when I saw the smug satisfaction on the prisoners' faces. The relief at escaping further horrors of war oozed from them. The wounded man looked at me and smiled.

'*Haben sie Wasser bitte*, Tommy?' he asked. That smile! How could he smile and ask for water when men all around him were being killed? Something in my head exploded.

'*Wasser*, I'll give you more than bloody *Wasser*, you grinning bastard,' I snarled. I was enraged and raising my Sten at him I squeezed the trigger, but a dozen flailing arms immediately crashed on to me, knocking the gun up, so that the shots ripped into the wall above the prisoners' heads, showering them with debris. I was slammed violently against the wall behind me and the impact seemed to bring me to my senses.

'What the bloody hell d'you think you're doing Whitey?' 'Christ Almighty Stan, calm down.' 'You of all people.' The angry admonishments came from all sides as my mates tried to pacify me. I felt cold and shivery but quickly calmed down as I focused on the prisoners, half-crouched, white-faced, fearfully eyeing the Sten I held across my chest.

'That bastard was laughing at me,' I muttered lamely.

'No he wasn't,' snapped one of the strangers sheltering with us. 'He asked for a drink of water. The smile was meant politely.' He was right. I had used the smile as an excuse to vent my overwhelming resentment on them. I was insanely jealous because they were all safe and the wounded man would be bathed and put in a clean bed, whereas I would be walking up that road soon into untold perils with my few remaining mates. Those were the thoughts that flashed through my mind, causing me to almost shoot a wounded prisoner. The shocked Germans were still eyeing me with horror and I felt ashamed at my outburst.

'I'll go to the O Group and get the gen,' I said, glad of an excuse to leave the house. Lieutenant Bernard was waiting for the NCOs in the cellar of a house a little further along.

'Righto you chaps,' he began. 'The reason we're setting off so quickly is because the Brass Hats want us to go at Jerry in short, sharp, jabbing attacks instead of the usual four- or five-mile push. We'll just do a mile or so and then another battalion will be coming through.' He gazed around at our numb expressions.

'So the rests will come quicker too,' he continued. 'We'll know further details when we hear how the 53rd Welsh get on. But we should be moving off in two or three hours, so tell your lads to get food inside them and some shut-eye.'

The little group began to disperse and I stood squinting at the platoon commander.

'What's up with you Whitey?' he asked.

'I believe you want to know who's going LOB sir.'

'Oh yes. They're very lucky whoever they are. Wish I was one of them,' he said.

'It's me and Beachy sir,' I blurted out. The officer looked stern.

'We can't send NCOs I'm afraid. You're needed here.' I knew I had a battle on my hands, but I was confident of winning. At that moment it would not have mattered if the officer confronting me had been a major, a colonel, Field Marshal Montgomery himself or the king. I had looked up the battle-scarred road ahead and in my tunnel vision it appeared as the gateway to hell. A premonition told me that if I took that journey I would not return alive.

'I'm an unpaid lance-corporal sir, and I've only had one LOB since the roster started six months ago. Some have had three and four turns.'

'Yes, but you were asked in turn and refused. It was your decision.'

'I know that sir, and I'm paying the price for it. I can't see properly. Everything's in tunnel vision and I'm useless like this.' He looked hard at me.

'Have you seen the MO?' I nodded.

'What did he say?'

'I'm just over-tired and over-stressed.'

'Is it right that you came over on D-Day when you were only seventeen?'

'That's right, sir, but I'm eighteen now.' He rubbed his chin.

'Did you know this was a seven-day LOB instead of the usual three?'

'No, sir, truthfully, I didn't. Why's that?'

'Because it's to Brussels, you lucky little bugger. A day to get there, five days in Brussels and a day to get back. So you and Beachy get scrubbed up and report to battalion HQ right away. But it's made things bloody awkward for me.' If peace had suddenly been declared I could not have felt more elated.

'Thank you very much sir,' I said, and against all protocol I grabbed the officer's hand and shook it vigorously.

'Go on, get off. See you in seven days,' he said grinning.

Naturally Beachy was equally excited and after the good luck wishes of the lads – and suspicious and envious glances from the newer members of the platoon – we hastened to battalion HQ to board the liberty truck bound for Brussels. Despite the bumpy ride we slept most of the way, to be roused by the driver at journey's end.

'Come on you dozy buggers,' he called. 'Are you getting off or do you want to stay on and I'll take you back?' Joke or not, it frightened us into jumping from the truck smartly. An efficient ladies' organization gave us a card and directed us to an address where, after a shower and a meal, we crawled between clean linen sheets and enjoyed a long, untroubled sleep.

Feeling invigorated, we set out to explore the city and were surprised to meet up with members of our old unit, the 1st Bucks Battalion, stationed in Brussels. During our chat I felt initial resentment and anger at the thought of our ex-buddies having fun in the bright lights while a day's ride away their compatriots were fighting and dying. Still, these lads were not running the show, I consoled myself, they just followed orders.

We dropped into the Monty Club at the Palais de Justice, a huge complex for the forces on leave, with restaurants and bars, swimming, dancing and other facilities. In the dancehall we sat at a table with beers and watched the dancers cavorting while a band blared out the hits of the day. (Luckily the long sleep had cured my tunnel vision.) It all seemed so unreal and I found it hard to adjust to the relaxed atmosphere. I was convinced I would wake up and be told to prepare for a night patrol. But it was real enough, as were the Waafs sitting at a nearby table. Beachy nudged me.

'I think the little one fancies you, Whitey.' I had only limited knowledge of the fair sex and my confidence was low. Nevertheless, as I looked over towards 'the little one' I felt an inner glow. She was smiling pleasantly and nodding her head in time to the music.

'For Christ's sake Whitey, what are you waiting for?' Beachy asked impatiently. I was so naive that her raised eyebrows meant nothing to me. But then her pretty little head inclined towards the dance floor and I got the message. I loved dancing but was wearing hobnailed boots, hardly suitable footwear for gliding over the polished floor. I returned the Waaf's smile and raised my boots to indicate my dilemma. She never lost her sweet smile as she stood up, eyes riveted to mine, and approached our table.

'Kick me with those bloody boots and I'll kick you back,' she said calmly, taking my hand and leading me on to the floor. Could this be happening to me? A few days ago I had been a babbling, bumbling, faint-hearted soldier ready to shoot prisoners and revile mates who were about to maim each other. Now I was floating on air in the arms of a saucy, perfumed, pretty girl in heavenly surroundings. No wonder I fell for Peggy, which I soon learned was her name. Beachy seemed happy with another Waaf and we all arranged to meet that evening.

I became enamoured of Peggy, who was twenty-one and had a pilot boyfriend somewhere. Our hours together that evening were romantic and passionate, though I was inexperienced in such matters and my strict upbringing decreed that sex was taboo between unmarried couples.

During the following days we had a glorious time in Brussels, enjoying the sights and sounds of a bustling city which, despite the war, or perhaps because of it, was heaving with humanity as servicemen and women from many countries were drawn towards it. In the evenings Peggy and her pal took us in hand, spoiling us with their attentions.

Our two lovely Waafs were on duty and unable to see us one evening so Beachy and I set out early to explore the city's lively haunts. In search of somewhere to eat we entered a high-class store, where a chic lady of fortyish, smartly dressed and with her hair in a bun, greeted us.

'Can I help you Tommies?' she asked in good English.

'We're looking for somewhere to eat,' said Beachy.

'Ah, I will show you,' she answered, 'but first I have

something to ask you. When the Tommies liberated our city we were not here to show our gratitude to British soldiers. Can we show how happy and grateful we are to you please?' We agreed, whereupon she picked up a phone and summoned her husband, apparently a big boss here. He approached us with extended hand.

'Hallo chaps, I'm Oscar. Thank you for listening to my wife Yvonne. She feels awful that we have not shown our gratitude to anyone for our liberation. Can you eat with us later tonight?' After some hesitation we said yes and Oscar gave us his address before escorting us to the coffee bar for a free snack.

'See you tonight at eight,' he said, shaking our hands again.

At eight sharp we rang the bell of a stylish apartment block and Yvonne, looking even more chic, opened the door.

'Welcome, welcome,' she beamed excitedly, escorting us into a birdcage lift that took us several floors up to a carpeted landing. There Oscar ushered us into a sumptuous apartment.

'Champagne, Louise,' he called to the kitchen, 'our guests are here.' We heard corks pop and then Louise glided in, carrying a tray of drinks. Everything about Louise glistened: her long, dark hair, her skin, her dress, the jewellery and accessories, all combining to present a vision of loveliness.

'This is Louise, my niece,' said Yvonne. 'She is beautiful, yes?'

'Don't embarrass me Auntie,' said Louise coyly. She sat on the arm of a chesterfield sofa, swinging shapely, nylon-clad legs that held me spellbound. Oscar saw my admiring glances.

'Beautiful legs, eh Stanley?' I blushed and they all laughed as I choked on my champagne in trying to hide my bashfulness.

A huge oval dish on the table was crammed with various meats and salads and foolishly Beachy and I dived in, eating as though this was our last meal on earth. Then we realized that it was only the starter, to be followed by turkey and all the trimmings. Wine flowed freely as we struggled manfully to tuck in, so that by the time the cheeses arrived we were bursting at the seams.

During the meal we learned that Oscar had been wounded in the earlier war and had spent two years recuperating in a Welsh hospital. He and Beachy were therefore on common ground. Louise, in her mid-twenties, I should think, had been married to a sailor for only a few months and was living in Antwerp when the Germans struck. Her husband and the rest of the crew had fled to England in their frigate.

By the time coffee and brandies arrived Beachy was wearing a silly grin and Oscar, muttering to himself, staggered from chair to chair before leaving the room.

'Everybody sleep here tonight,' shouted Yvonne, flapping her arms. 'We all too zigzag tonight.' You can say that again lady, I thought as the room started to revolve, accelerating if I closed my eyes. I kept seeing the pretty, laughing face of Louise and yearned to talk more with her, but I would have to sober up a little first. By this time Beachy was sound asleep on a sofa, snoring contentedly. I groped my way to the bathroom and splashed cold water on my face and neck. Feeling a little better I opened the bathroom door and there stood Louise before me – naked. I thought I was dreaming until she took my hand and backed into an adjacent bedroom.

'Come Stanley, in here is bed. Off this, off this.' She tugged at my shirt and trousers and in record time I had stripped. She kissed my mouth, my face, my body from tip to toe, all the time gasping: 'You same to me Stanley, same to me.' I complied with gusto, thinking how much better it would be if only the room stopped spinning. She soon sensed my fumbling, inexperienced hands.

'Ah, for you this is first time, I think, eh Stanley?' she asked, sounding surprised. I was not embarrassed by the question, the drink having given me Dutch courage, or rather Belgian courage.

'Yep Louise,' I answered. 'Go easy with me.'

'Don't worry, I show you how … everyt'ing.' She held me tight, trying to suffocate me with kisses and then proceeded to the end of the lesson, gently and considerately. It was sheer bliss and after the last rapturous gasp I promptly fell asleep, only to be awoken several times during the night.

'Come to me Stanley,' she murmured, 'my 'usband you see 'as been away a long, long time.' Each time I would perform to the best of my ability.

'No, no, Stanley,' she would chide softly. 'Slowly, slowly. Ah! That's good,' my lovely tutor would gasp, whereupon I would fall asleep again.

During our last session, shortly before dawn, there was a loud bump in the lounge. Beachy had fallen off the sofa.

'Oh, what is that?' asked Louise, startled.

'It's your husband,' I said quickly. We both giggled uncontrollably to round off my beautiful education.

The next morning I awoke to find Yvonne shaking me.

'Coffee, Stanley?' she asked, smiling as ever. I looked round the room.

'Louise had to leave early for Antwerp,' she added hastily. 'She said for me to say thank you, she enjoyed meeting you both.' I smiled as I recalled our bedroom frolics and considered myself lucky to have been taught by such a stunning lady. Wait till I tell Beachy, I thought as I dressed. My mate and Oscar were in the kitchen, looking as though they had spent the night adrift in an open boat.

We thanked our hosts for a wonderful evening and exchanged addresses, promising to visit them again if we survived the war.

Ten years later we did call again, to find Oscar and Yvonne well, though the former had been advised to drink less. By now our hosts were retired and living in a smaller, but equally elegant flat. The meal was identical to the one we had enjoyed in 1945, though we were wiser now and paced ourselves more sensibly. Returning home on the boat Beachy turned to me.

'A pity we didn't see their niece. What was her name again?'

'Louise,' I answered.

'Ah yes, Louise. Of course you would remember, wouldn't you,' he laughed.

For the past fifty years I have exchanged Christmas cards with our Belgian friends, though sadly, but not surprisingly, Oscar recently succumbed to cirrhosis of the liver. However, Yvonne, now well over ninety, continues hale and hearty.

Beachy and I had a pleasant surprise when our good pal Shorty appeared at the Monty Club on a short leave, and we tarried several more days so that we could all return together.

Our Brussels sojourn simply flew and saying farewell to Peggy was heartbreaking and distressing. I had grown very fond of her, despite my brief, exhilarating initiation with Louise, and she obviously had strong feelings for me, though she needed time to sort herself out. The first few hours of that bumpy return journey were spent reliving Brussels' delights, after which we dozed while the truck rumbled northwards.

'Who's for a gipsy's kiss?' shouted the driver, rousing us as he pulled into a field. We all jumped out, glad to be able to stretch our legs, and as I glanced around I noticed the landscape had changed dramatically, with military hardware all around us and squaddies' faces looking grim and careworn. I was back in the world I knew best, the world of killing and barbarity; Brussels was but a dream. A familiar chill crept over me, causing sweat to moisten my armpits, my palms and the small of my back. I felt cold and on fire at the same time. Beachy shuddered visibly, indicating that fear was also striking into his very bones, and even the normally imperturbable Shorty had a forlorn look.

Back in the truck we were quieter, each of us trying to hide his thoughts and fears as the 'business end' drew ominously near. My apprehension mounted to such an extent that I felt depressed, and although no longer a firm believer in the Almighty, I found myself half-praying, half-wishing that the truck would run off the road and put us in hospital, where at least we would be free from the insidious, gnawing fear that increased alarmingly with each passing mile. I wondered anxiously whether I could stomach another spell up front without completely breaking down or doing something rash. Our conversation became forced, and to stop our minds dwelling on our ultimate destination we spoke bitterly of the 'good-time soldiers' doing their war service in Brussels or Antwerp. It seemed unfair that nine-tenths of the army should be soldiering in comparative luxury while the other tenth, the 'cutting edge', were being killed, badly maimed or mentally ground into nervous wrecks. We agreed that all servicemen, from clerks to cooks, drivers to storemen, should spend a week in the front line so that they could understand what we had to endure day and night, week after week.

The last few miles were another world: burnt-out roadside tanks – both ours and the enemy's; temporary little burial plots with a pathetic collection of clumsy crosses leaning at crazy angles; and blasted, smoke-blackened buildings bordering the lanes. Why were we returning to this torture? After ten punishing months we were challenging the law of averages, having lost so many of our mates since the long haul from Normandy's beaches.

We faced the uncertain future with grave doubts, although by now the enemy were showing distinct signs of weakening and I was confident that the war in Europe had but a short term to run. In fact, with Russian hordes pressing relentlessly from the east, and the Western Allies continuing their vigorous push, the once-invincible Wehrmacht was being squeezed in a gigantic nutcracker. Within a few short weeks the Third Reich, which Hitler had boasted would last for a thousand years, was vanquished and lay in ruins, never to rise again.

I was sentenced to twenty-eight days' detention for overstaying my Brussels leave, but this probably saved my life because I missed the Rhine crossing during which, at the small German town of Speldrop, my old platoon was ambushed and virtually wiped out, though my best pal Shorty escaped unhurt.

At the end of hostilities in Europe I was unexpectedly asked if I was afraid of snakes and told that I was being shipped to the Far East to face the Japanese. *En route* to that theatre the Japanese surrendered; nevertheless, I spent two eventful years out east – a year in Burma and a year in Malaya chasing 'commie rebels' – before returning home. On 25 October 1947 I was hugging my mum and sister Edith in our tiny living-room.

'We've got your twenty-first birthday organized for the day after tomorrow,' said my mum through her tears.

'You'll be a man then, Stanno,' Edith piped up.

'He's been a man for the last five years, haven't you son?' said mum hugging me tightly.

Appendix: Sword Beach – British Plan of Attack

For the successful development of the British plan of attack the left flank had to be securely protected. The Caen Canal and the River Orne provided an ideal anti-tank obstacle and the general assault was to be preceded during the night of D−1 by the landing of troops of the 6th Airborne Division to secure these waterway bridges, seize the high ground to the east and silence a battery of heavy guns near Franceville Plage.

The 3rd British Division's assault was to be led by DD (Duplex-Drive) tanks of the 27th Armoured Brigade, which would deal with any guns not silenced by the air and naval bombardments. Five minutes later AVREs (Armoured Vehicles, Royal Engineers) were to land and blast a way through any obstacles barring progress inland.

The first wave of assaulting infantry, the 8th Infantry Brigade, followed closely behind and was given the task of mopping up the beach garrisons and securing the high ground at Periers-sur-Dan. The 4th Commando was to mop up Ouistreham and secure the locks at the mouth of the Caen Canal, while 41st Royal Marine Commando captured Lion-sur-Mer and Luc-sur-Mer and 44th Commando, landing with the Canadians, moved east and joined them. Both would then secure Douvres-la-Delivrande.

In No. 101 Beach Area, No. 5 Beach Group would land with the assaulting brigade on the first tide to develop the beaches and establish sector stores dumps. No. 6 Beach Group would land on the second tide and establish the beach maintenance area, or carry out contingency plans. When fully deployed No. 5 Beach Group would work the beaches and No. 6 Beach Group would work the beach maintenance area.

An advance party of No. 6 Beach Group was to land on the first tide and reconnoitre the beach maintenance area as soon as possible. Its commander would then report to the beach group commander, who would land with the main body, thus enabling the latter to make adjustments to the key plan before the main body was deployed. The anti-tank platoon was also to land on the first tide and deploy immediately.

On landing on the second tide the main body of No. 6 Beach Group would form in transit areas to await further orders.

Role allotted to the 1st Bucks Battalion:

Battalion HQ – Command of No. 6 Beach Group.

A and B Companies – Beach companies opening new beaches on landing.

C Company – In support of ammunition/ordnance dumps.

D Company – Reserve Company.

S Company:
    Anti-tank Platoon – Anti-tank defence of area.
    Mortar Platoon – Organization of unaccompanied stores dump.
    Carrier Platoon – In support of supplies dump.

H Company:
    Signal Platoon – Beach signals.
    Pioneer Platoon – Mine clearance and construction of HQ No. 6 Beach Group.

In addition to stores (mostly ammunition) landed early, one hundred 10 cwt trailers of ammunition were to be taken ashore by the beach troops.

In the event of the enemy's 14-inch guns at Le Havre not being silenced, an alternative plan was for No. 6 Beach Group's barges to land on the 3rd Canadian Division's sector (Juno Beach), from where stores would be ferried overland to the original beach maintenance area.